# THE DARK SIDE

WRITTEN BY DANIEL LIPKOWITZ

# CONTENTS

# INTRODUCTION

## Fear. Anger. Hate. Suffering.

There are many pathways to the dark side of the Force. For some, this journey begins with rage and greed. The dark side grants its users great power, but it also twists their bodies and minds, turning them into servants of destruction.

The Sith have long used the dark side to accomplish their sinister aims. One Sith Lord, called Darth Sidious, transformed a peaceful Republic into a violent Empire. He turned a Jedi hero into his cruel apprentice. And he nearly destroyed the Jedi Order, the one thing that could bring an end to his evil.

You don't know the power of the dark side.

### But soon, you will.

---

**NOTE ON DATES**

Dates are fixed around the Battle of Yavin in year 0.
The dates recorded in this book are measured in terms
of years Before (BBY) and After (ABY) the Battle of Yavin,
when the first Death Star was destroyed by Luke Skywalker.

# CHAPTER ONE
# THE REPUBLIC ERA

It is a time of peace for the glorious Galactic Republic. Its citizens have not known warfare in centuries, and any disputes that arise are easily settled by the brave knights of the Jedi Order.

But the dark side is stirring. The ancient, evil Sith are not extinct as the Jedi believe. Controlled by the mysterious Darth Sidious, powerful groups try to break away from the Republic, creating great unrest and turmoil throughout the galaxy…

AT LAST WE WILL REVEAL OURSELVES TO THE JEDI.

AT LAST WE WILL SHOW OFF THESE AWESOME TATTOOS.

# DARTH SIDIOUS

**ALTHOUGH THE EVIL** Sith are thought to be long gone, one has survived. Lurking behind the scenes, he has secretly manipulated the Republic, the Separatists and even the Jedi to fulfil his goals of conquest and revenge. To most, he is Palpatine… but his Sith name is Darth Sidious.

Eyes corrupted by dark side power

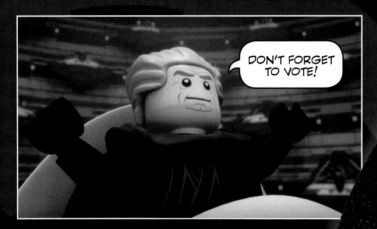

DON'T FORGET TO VOTE!

### RISE TO POWER
At first, Palpatine appears to be a kind and humble senator from the planet Naboo. Through clever scheming, he is elected Chancellor of the entire Republic. Finally, he declares himself Emperor – the tyrannical leader of the new Galactic Empire!

### EMPEROR PALPATINE
As Emperor, Sidious rules the galaxy through strength and fear. He does not care about crowns or fancy clothes, preferring to sit in the shadows and plot the destruction of all who oppose him. He does not believe that anything will ever topple his power.

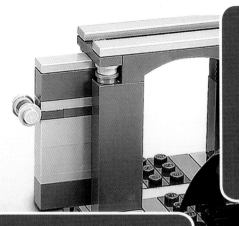

## A CRUEL MASTER

Being Sidious's Sith apprentice is not an easy job. The hard work, cruel punishments for failure and constant training are bad enough… but he's also always on the lookout for someone even stronger to replace you!

R-REALLY, MASTER – A WOOKIEE ATE MY HOMEWORK!

## EVIL REVEALED

When the Jedi finally suspect Palpatine's true identity as a Sith Lord, they try to arrest him. Instead, Darth Sidious turns the tables and defeats them all – with the help of his newest apprentice, Darth Vader!

Force lightning

Chancellor's office

Jedi Master Mace Windu

Shadowy black robes

## DATA FILE

 **HOMEWORLD:** NABOO

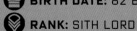 **BIRTH DATE:** 82 BBY

**RANK:** SITH LORD

 **TRAINED BY:** DARTH PLAGUEIS

 **WEAPON:** RED-BLADED LIGHTSABER, FORCE LIGHTNING

**❝EVERYTHING IS PROCEEDING AS I HAVE FORESEEN.❞**
DARTH SIDIOUS

# TWO SIDES OF

THE FORCE IS A mysterious, invisible energy that surrounds everything in the galaxy. The Sith follow the dark side of the Force, which teaches them to embrace anger, selfishness and power. The Jedi Knights follow the light side and learn calmness and compassion. Every Force user sees the Force differently!

THE FORCE IS PRESENT IN EVERY LIVING THING. IF WE LISTEN CAREFULLY, WE CAN LEARN FROM IT.

Qui-Gon Jinn believes in the Living Force.

THE FORCE CAN LET YOU SENSE DISTANT EVENTS AND FRIENDS, AND EVEN GLIMPSE THE FUTURE.

Yoda is one of the wisest and strongest Force users of all time.

THE FORCE BRINGS VICTORY IN BATTLE, AND PEACE AND JUSTICE TO THE GALAXY.

Mace Windu is a great warrior and lightsaber master.

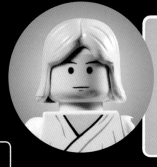

THE FORCE IS KIND OF CONFUSING, BUT HANDY FOR GETTING OUT OF A JAM.

Luke Skywalker has much to learn about the Jedi path.

THE FORCE SHOULD BE USED WITH PATIENCE AND THOUGHTFULNESS.

Obi-Wan Kenobi is a disciplined and experienced Jedi.

# THE FORCE

Followers of the **Unifying Force** philosophy believe that there is no real **light** side or **dark** side, but only different ways of **using** the Force.

POWER IS ALL THAT MATTERS. AND THE FORCE IS THE ULTIMATE SOURCE OF POWER.

Darth Sidious craves only one thing.

THE FORCE HELPS YOU KEEP THOSE AROUND YOU FRIGHTENED AND OBEDIENT.

Darth Vader wants order in the galaxy at any cost.

THE FORCE LETS YOU CONTROL THE MEEK, THE FOOLISH AND THE WEAK-WILLED.

Darth Tyranus manipulates others to serve his goals.

THE FORCE IS A TOOL FOR GETTING YOUR REVENGE.

Asajj Ventress is driven by rage.

THE FORCE LETS YOU BE BETTER THAN EVERYBODY ELSE.

Darth Maul always needs to win.

### JEDI AND SITH
Which side of the Force is more powerful? The Sith believe that the dark side is stronger, and see the Jedi as weaklings. But while the dark side grants its users incredible strength, the Jedi train hard in the light side – and are often able to defeat a Sith who has chosen the quicker and easier path to power.

# JEDI ORDER

Many **Sith** were once Jedi who **turned** to the dark side and **abandoned** the vows and teachings of the **Jedi Order**.

## JEDI KNIGHTS

The Jedi are protectors of peace, but they are also skilled warriors who are ready to raise their lightsabers to combat evil. During the Clone Wars, Jedi Generals join forces to protect the Republic.

COLEMAN TREBOR

OBI-WAN KENOBI

SHAAK TI

HERE WE ARE, TO SAVE THE DAY!

BARRISS OFFEE

LUMINARA UNDULI

AGEN KOLAR

KIT FISTO

**FOR TENS OF THOUSANDS** of years, the Jedi Order has gathered together Force users from every intelligent species in the galaxy to safeguard harmony and justice. The Jedi are peacemakers, law keepers and defenders of those who cannot defend themselves. They are the greatest enemy of the dark side.

## HOLOCRON VAULT

Inside the Jedi Temple on Coruscant is the fabled Holocron vault. Each Holocron information crystal contains a precious collection of Jedi knowledge. The Holocrons hold many centuries of the Order's history… and all of its secrets, too, making the Holocrons a much-desired prize for the Sith.

## JEDI TECHNOLOGY

As protectors of the Republic, the Jedi fly starships that are built using the latest technology. Although some starfighters, such as Obi-Wan's Eta-2 Interceptor, are too small to be fitted with a hyperdrive of their own, the Republic have many hyperdrive rings, which can launch smaller ships into hyperspace.

## DARK JEDI

Every so often, a Jedi may find himself tempted by the dark side. Jedi General Pong Krell has a dangerous craving for power – and he embraces the dark side to get it. During the Battle of Umbara, Krell sabotages his own troops to thwart the Republic's war effort. Such treachery allows Krell to join the ranks of other fallen Jedi, such as Count Dooku and Anakin Skywalker.

LET'S PUT OUR TROOPS RIGHT IN THE LINE OF FIRE.

UMM, OKAY...

Wise and kindly face

Rare purple lightsaber blade

Traditional Jedi robes

YODA

MACE WINDU

## DATA FILE

- **LEADER:** YODA
- **FOUNDED IN:** 25,000 BBY
- **MISSION:** PROMOTE PEACE AND PROTECT THE GALAXY

## JEDI MASTERS

In the late days of the Republic, the two most important Jedi Masters are Yoda and Mace Windu. Although each has his own unique style of leading, both are committed to destroying the last remaining Sith. Unfortunately for them, the Sith strike first!

# GLORY OF THE OLD SITH EMPIRE

"WHO NEEDS A HELMET WHEN YOU'VE GOT GOOD LOOKS LIKE THESE?"

Breathing mask

**DARTH SIDIOUS AND** Darth Vader are far from the first dark side users to call themselves Lords of the Sith. Thousands of years earlier, there was an entire empire ruled by fearsome Sith Lords. This Sith Empire was powerful enough to rival the old Republic.

Sith Raider armour

## DARTH MALGUS

Darth Malgus was a lord in the Sith Empire. He was injured in battle and had to wear a respirator mask to survive. Believing that the Sith Empire was too weak, Malgus wanted to create a new and even stronger empire of his own.

### SITH SOLDIERS

Fuelled by hatred and rage, dark side warriors of the Sith Empire and the armoured troopers who served them sought out the empire's enemies and destroyed any opposition to its rule.

Protective combat padding

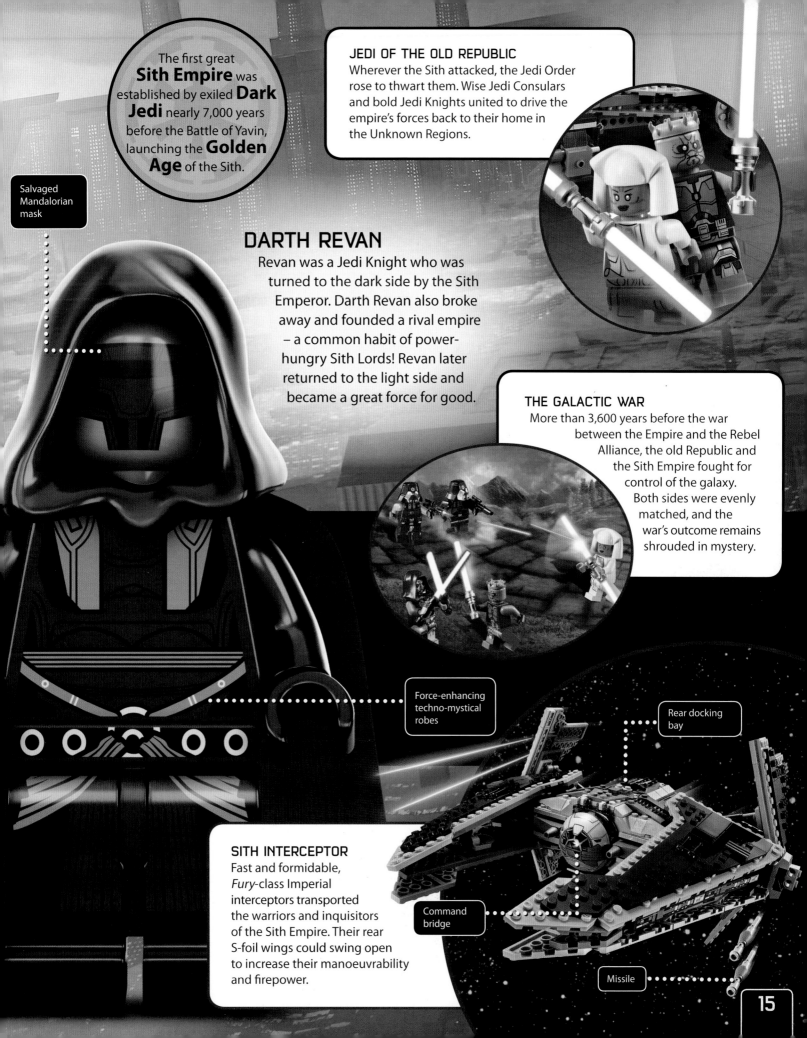

The first great **Sith Empire** was established by exiled **Dark Jedi** nearly 7,000 years before the Battle of Yavin, launching the **Golden Age** of the Sith.

Salvaged Mandalorian mask

## JEDI OF THE OLD REPUBLIC
Wherever the Sith attacked, the Jedi Order rose to thwart them. Wise Jedi Consulars and bold Jedi Knights united to drive the empire's forces back to their home in the Unknown Regions.

## DARTH REVAN
Revan was a Jedi Knight who was turned to the dark side by the Sith Emperor. Darth Revan also broke away and founded a rival empire – a common habit of power-hungry Sith Lords! Revan later returned to the light side and became a great force for good.

## THE GALACTIC WAR
More than 3,600 years before the war between the Empire and the Rebel Alliance, the old Republic and the Sith Empire fought for control of the galaxy. Both sides were evenly matched, and the war's outcome remains shrouded in mystery.

Force-enhancing techno-mystical robes

Rear docking bay

## SITH INTERCEPTOR
Fast and formidable, *Fury*-class Imperial interceptors transported the warriors and inquisitors of the Sith Empire. Their rear S-foil wings could swing open to increase their manoeuvrability and firepower.

Command bridge

Missile

15

Head and body covered in tattoos

Zabrak horns

## DATA FILE

- **HOMEWORLD:** DATHOMIR
- **BIRTH DATE:** 54 BBY
- **RANK:** SITH LORD
- **TRAINED BY:** DARTH SIDIOUS
- **WEAPON:** RED DOUBLE-BLADED LIGHTSABER

Darksaber of defeated Mandalorian leader

# DARTH MAUL

**SOMETIMES, THE SITH** need to use cunning and subtlety. Other times, they just want a blunt instrument. Darth Maul may not be the most clever or sneaky of dark side warriors, but his strength and rage make him a huge danger to the Jedi – and the perfect first apprentice for Darth Sidious.

Cybernetic legs

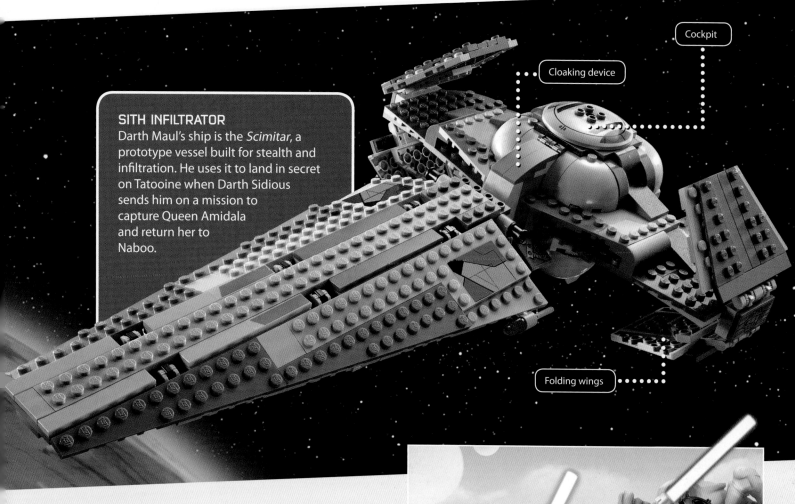

Cockpit

Cloaking device

Folding wings

### SITH INFILTRATOR
Darth Maul's ship is the *Scimitar*, a prototype vessel built for stealth and infiltration. He uses it to land in secret on Tatooine when Darth Sidious sends him on a mission to capture Queen Amidala and return her to Naboo.

### MAUL'S REVENGE
Even the loss of his entire lower body cannot put an end to Darth Maul. Years after his apparent death, he returns with a set of mechanical legs and takes over the planet Mandalore – until his rebellion is put to an end by his former Master, Darth Sidious.

> **"AT LAST WE WILL REVEAL OURSELVES TO THE JEDI. AT LAST WE WILL HAVE REVENGE."**
> DARTH MAUL

BOO! SURPRISE SITH ATTACK!

### LOOK AT ME!
Darth Maul might have been defeated by the Jedi, but he is still a bit of a show off. After the destruction of the first Death Star, Darth Maul and Darth Vader find themselves competing for the Emperor's approval – and Maul can't resist demonstrating his awesome new eight-bladed lightsaber!

### FIRST CONTACT
There has been no sign of the Sith for centuries – until now! When Qui-Gon Jinn travels to Tatooine with Obi-Wan and Queen Amidala, a sinister cloaked figure reveals himself as Darth Maul, an unknown Sith apprentice. Qui-Gon must act fast to protect Queen Amidala. He battles fiercely against the Sith, but only a well-timed jump into Amidala's starship saves the Jedi Master.

# CAN A SITH APPRENTICE BE DEFEATED?

**THE FULLY UNLEASHED** power of the dark side has not been faced by the Jedi in many lifetimes. Now that Darth Maul has revealed himself, is there a Jedi in the galaxy who is brave enough to take a stand against his vengeful rage?

### FEARLESS SITH
Darth Maul is a fearless warrior. He has used his powers of intimidation to help invade the peaceful planet of Naboo. When Jedi Master Qui-Gon Jinn and his Padawan apprentice, Obi-Wan Kenobi, confront Maul, he is more than ready to battle. To the surprise of his Jedi foes, Maul's lightsaber ignites with not one, but two deadly red blades.

### A CLASH OF THE FORCE
Qui-Gon Jinn believes that the Force is an energy present in all living things. When laser walls separate Qui-Gon from Maul, the Jedi meditates to become one with the light side. Maul, eager to battle, paces impatiently, waiting for the walls to vanish. When the calm of the light side and the ferocity of the dark side come face to face, which will triumph?

C'MO-O-ON, LET'S FIGHT ALREADY!

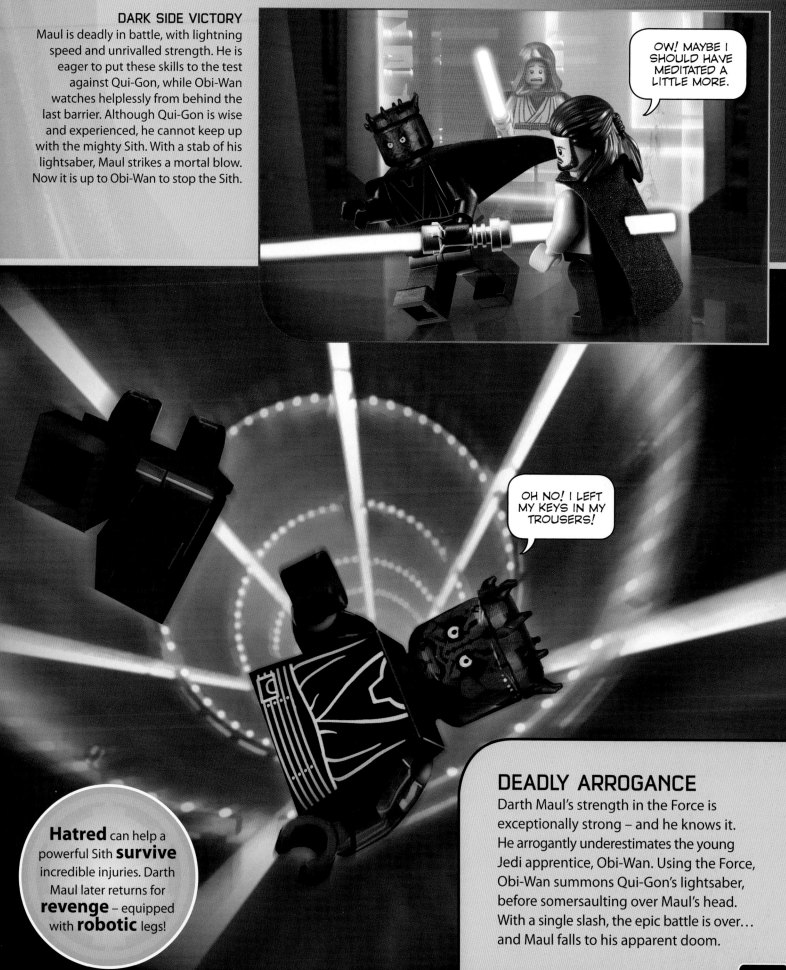

## DARK SIDE VICTORY

Maul is deadly in battle, with lightning speed and unrivalled strength. He is eager to put these skills to the test against Qui-Gon, while Obi-Wan watches helplessly from behind the last barrier. Although Qui-Gon is wise and experienced, he cannot keep up with the mighty Sith. With a stab of his lightsaber, Maul strikes a mortal blow. Now it is up to Obi-Wan to stop the Sith.

OW! MAYBE I SHOULD HAVE MEDITATED A LITTLE MORE.

OH NO! I LEFT MY KEYS IN MY TROUSERS!

**Hatred** can help a powerful Sith **survive** incredible injuries. Darth Maul later returns for **revenge** – equipped with **robotic** legs!

## DEADLY ARROGANCE

Darth Maul's strength in the Force is exceptionally strong – and he knows it. He arrogantly underestimates the young Jedi apprentice, Obi-Wan. Using the Force, Obi-Wan summons Qui-Gon's lightsaber, before somersaulting over Maul's head. With a single slash, the epic battle is over… and Maul falls to his apparent doom.

19

# DARTH SIDIOUS'S

JEDI KNIGHTS CARRY THEIR lightsabers with them wherever they go, but it's not so easy when you're a secret Sith Lord pretending to be a friendly politician. While posing as the peaceful Chancellor Palpatine, Darth Sidious makes sure that his extravagant lightsaber is never too far away. He cleverly keeps it hidden in a place he can reach in a hurry.

Sidious **hides** his finely crafted lightsaber inside a **statue** in the Chancellor's office. When he uses the Force to **activate** its blade, it **burns** its own way out!

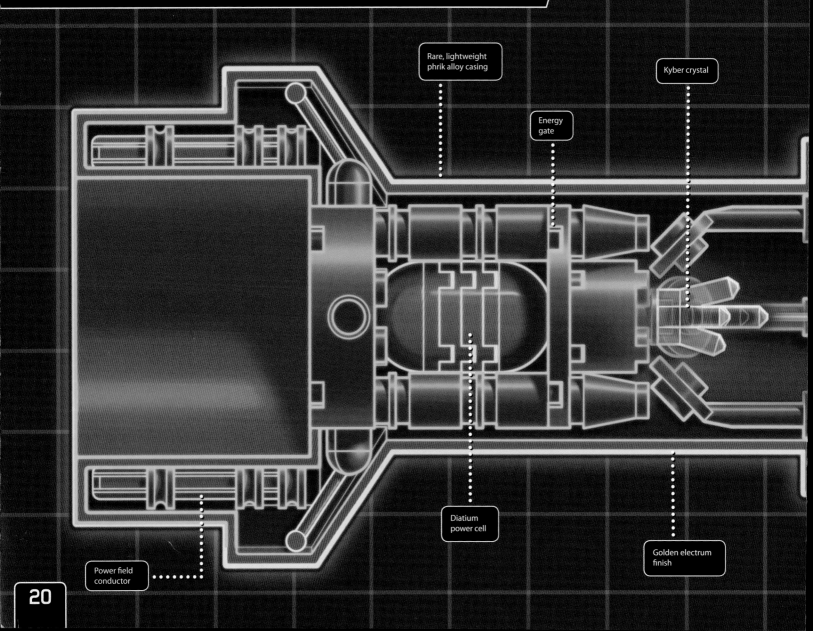

Rare, lightweight phrik alloy casing

Energy gate

Kyber crystal

Diatium power cell

Golden electrum finish

Power field conductor

# LIGHTSABER

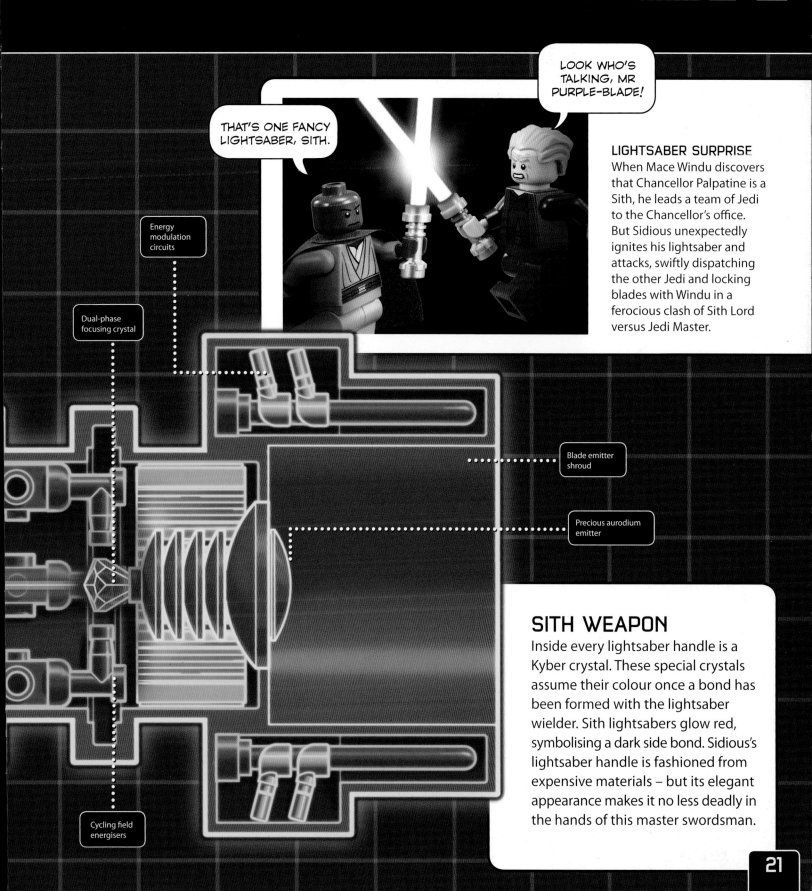

THAT'S ONE FANCY LIGHTSABER, SITH.

LOOK WHO'S TALKING, MR PURPLE-BLADE!

Energy modulation circuits

Dual-phase focusing crystal

Blade emitter shroud

Precious aurodium emitter

Cycling field energisers

## LIGHTSABER SURPRISE
When Mace Windu discovers that Chancellor Palpatine is a Sith, he leads a team of Jedi to the Chancellor's office. But Sidious unexpectedly ignites his lightsaber and attacks, swiftly dispatching the other Jedi and locking blades with Windu in a ferocious clash of Sith Lord versus Jedi Master.

## SITH WEAPON
Inside every lightsaber handle is a Kyber crystal. These special crystals assume their colour once a bond has been formed with the lightsaber wielder. Sith lightsabers glow red, symbolising a dark side bond. Sidious's lightsaber handle is fashioned from expensive materials – but its elegant appearance makes it no less deadly in the hands of this master swordsman.

# DARTH TYRANUS

**PUBLICLY KNOWN AS** Count Dooku, Darth Sidious's second apprentice is a very different sort of Sith from Darth Maul. A born aristocrat and once a great Jedi Master, Tyranus is intelligent and charismatic, but with a streak of arrogance that leads him to quit the Jedi Order and join the dark side.

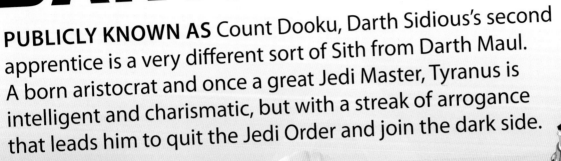

Handlebars control altitude

Republic gunship in pursuit

*BEEP BEEP! IMPORTANT SITH COMING THROUGH!*

Rear stabiliser fin

Forward-mounted driver's seat

**GEONOSIS CHASE**
Although he is supremely confident in his own abilities, Darth Tyranus is shrewd enough to retreat when his Master's plans demand it. As the Jedi arrive on the Separatist planet of Geonosis with their new Clone Army, Tyranus zooms away aboard his Flitknot speeder.

**SEPARATIST LEADER**
Using his well-known identity as the influential Count Dooku, Tyranus convinces unhappy members of the Republic such as the Geonosians and the Trade Federation to revolt against the Republic, starting the Clone Wars. Tyranus's Separatist allies believe he will lead them to victory, but it is secretly all part of a plot to give the Sith control over the galaxy.

*THIS SEEMS LIKE A GOOD IDEA.*

*YES, A VERY GOOD IDEA!*

Not only was Count Dooku a **respected** Jedi before he became a **Sith**, but he was also the teacher of Obi-Wan Kenobi's Master, **Qui-Gon Jinn**.

Elegantly trimmed facial hair

Cloak provides a hint of menace

## DATA FILE

 **HOMEWORLD:** SERENNO

 **BIRTH DATE:** 102 BBY

 **RANK:** SITH LORD, FORMER JEDI MASTER

**TRAINED BY:** YODA, DARTH SIDIOUS

**WEAPON:** RED-BLADED LIGHTSABER

> ❝I'VE BECOME MORE **POWERFUL** THAN ANY JEDI.❞
> DARTH TYRANUS

Curved lightsaber hilt

## FALLEN JEDI
As a Jedi, Count Dooku excelled at lightsaber fencing and moving objects with the Force, but he grew discontented with the Jedi Council and the Republic. As a Sith, Darth Tyranus cruelly enjoys deceiving his would-be friends and blasting his enemies with sizzling Force lightning.

# CAN ONE SITH DEFEAT THREE JEDI?

### YOUNG AND RECKLESS

Anakin is a reckless Jedi. Despite Obi-Wan's warnings to be careful, Anakin charges straight for Tyranus. Before Anakin's lightsaber can even touch him, Tyranus blasts him with Force lightning, hurling the brash young Jedi aside. Tyranus tries the same manoeuvre on Obi-Wan, but the experienced Jedi blocks the attack with his blade.

### TWO AGAINST ONE

The battle between the dark side and the light side begins. Obi-Wan is good, but the powerful Sith is better. As Tyranus prepares to strike the final, fatal blow, Anakin leaps back into the fight to protect his Master and friend. But even armed with two lightsabers, Anakin cannot beat Tyranus – and he loses an arm for his trouble.

**THE SITH BELIEVE** the dark side of the Force offers more power to its users than the light side. Darth Tyranus puts this theory to the test when his escape from the planet Geonosis is interrupted by three Jedi: Anakin Skywalker, Obi-Wan Kenobi and Yoda.

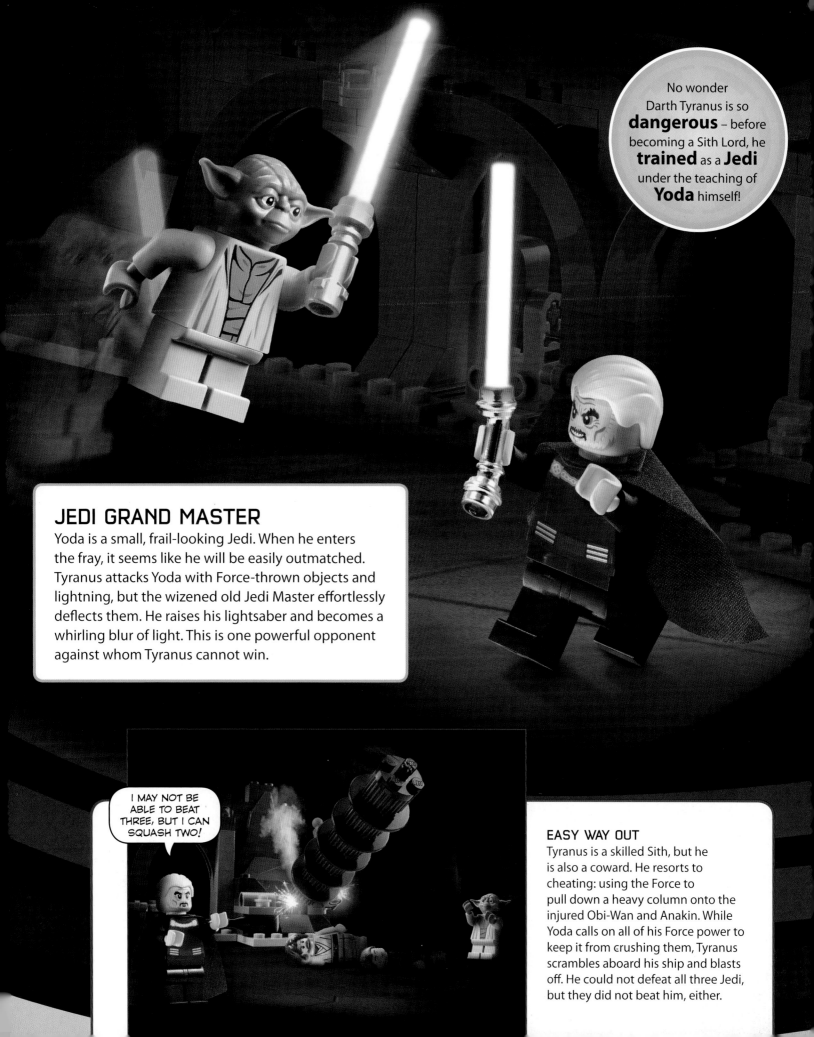

No wonder Darth Tyranus is so **dangerous** – before becoming a Sith Lord, he **trained** as a **Jedi** under the teaching of **Yoda** himself!

## JEDI GRAND MASTER

Yoda is a small, frail-looking Jedi. When he enters the fray, it seems like he will be easily outmatched. Tyranus attacks Yoda with Force-thrown objects and lightning, but the wizened old Jedi Master effortlessly deflects them. He raises his lightsaber and becomes a whirling blur of light. This is one powerful opponent against whom Tyranus cannot win.

I MAY NOT BE ABLE TO BEAT THREE, BUT I CAN SQUASH TWO!

## EASY WAY OUT

Tyranus is a skilled Sith, but he is also a coward. He resorts to cheating: using the Force to pull down a heavy column onto the injured Obi-Wan and Anakin. While Yoda calls on all of his Force power to keep it from crushing them, Tyranus scrambles aboard his ship and blasts off. He could not defeat all three Jedi, but they did not beat him, either.

# CHAPTER TWO
# THE CLONE WARS ERA

While the starfighters of the Republic and the Separatists clash in battle, while legions of clone troopers fight against battalions of battle droids on countless war-torn worlds, Darth Sidious watches and knows that his victory is inevitable.

As Chancellor, he commands the Republic army, and through his dark side servants, he controls the Separatist forces as well. No matter which side wins the Clone Wars, Sidious shall triumph – and the Jedi Knights will lose…

MWA HA HA! IT'S ALL GOING ACCORDING TO PLAN.

# ASAJJ VENTRESS

**ASAJJ VENTRESS HAS** everything she needs to be a Sith, except for opportunity. As Darth Tyranus's Sith student, she learns the ways of the dark side, but can never become a true apprentice while there are already two Sith Lords in the galaxy.

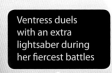
Ventress duels with an extra lightsaber during her fiercest battles

Tattoos of vengeance

HERE'S WHAT YOU'LL GET IF YOU BEAT ME AT HOLOCHESS AGAIN!

## SITH MASTER
When they first meet, Ventress thinks she knows more about the dark side than Darth Tyranus does. A blast of Force lightning quickly teaches her otherwise, and she becomes his disciple and personal assassin.

## DATA FILE

 **HOMEWORLD:** DATHOMIR

 **BIRTH DATE:** 47 BBY

 **RANK:** DARK APPRENTICE

 **TRAINED BY:** DARTH TYRANUS

 **WEAPON:** TWIN RED-BLADED LIGHTSABERS

## NIGHTSISTER
Born into the witch-like Nightsisters of Dathomir, Ventress was once trained as a Jedi, but fell to the dark side. She chooses to work for Darth Tyranus in exchange for his Sith teachings and soon becomes known as a ruthless threat to the Jedi Order.

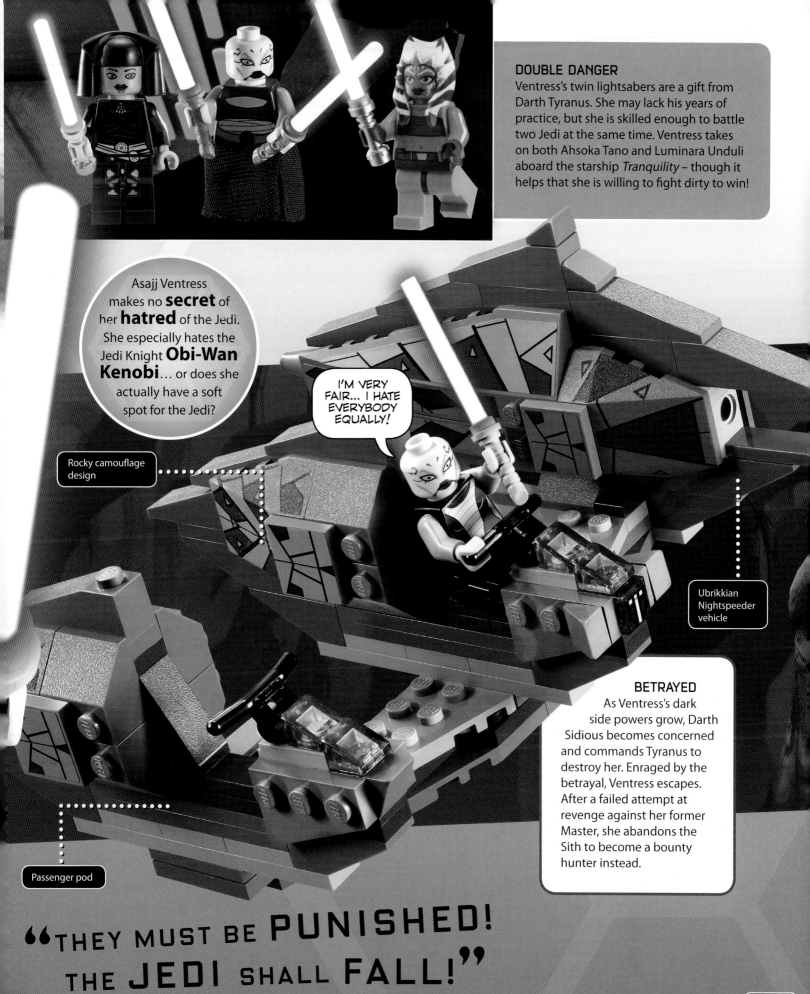

## DOUBLE DANGER
Ventress's twin lightsabers are a gift from Darth Tyranus. She may lack his years of practice, but she is skilled enough to battle two Jedi at the same time. Ventress takes on both Ahsoka Tano and Luminara Unduli aboard the starship *Tranquility* – though it helps that she is willing to fight dirty to win!

Asajj Ventress makes no **secret** of her **hatred** of the Jedi. She especially hates the Jedi Knight **Obi-Wan Kenobi**… or does she actually have a soft spot for the Jedi?

I'M VERY FAIR... I HATE EVERYBODY EQUALLY!

Rocky camouflage design

Ubrikkian Nightspeeder vehicle

## BETRAYED
As Ventress's dark side powers grow, Darth Sidious becomes concerned and commands Tyranus to destroy her. Enraged by the betrayal, Ventress escapes. After a failed attempt at revenge against her former Master, she abandons the Sith to become a bounty hunter instead.

Passenger pod

## "THEY MUST BE PUNISHED! THE JEDI SHALL FALL!"
ASAJJ VENTRESS

29

# SITH APPRENTICES

**ACCORDING TO THE** ancient Rule of Two, only two Sith Lords may co-exist. If a Sith Master senses someone with strong dark side potential, he may take on an apprentice. But he should proceed with caution – an apprentice is just one treacherous step away from becoming the next Master!

> DON'T GET ANY CLEVER IDEAS, KID.

The **Rule of Two** was created by **Darth Bane**, a Sith Lord from 1,000 years before Darth Sidious's **time**. He was tired of the galaxy's many **Sith** endlessly fighting each other for power.

## MASTER AND APPRENTICE
Darth Sidious was still the apprentice of Darth Plagueis "the Wise" when he started training Darth Maul. By the time Darth Vader becomes the new apprentice, Plagueis is no more and Sidious is the Master.

## SITH TRAINING
A Sith apprentice's training involves discomfort, deprivation and sacrifice, all intended to make the apprentice rely on the dark side of the Force. Darth Tyranus shows no mercy during the training of his new apprentice, Darth Maul's brother Savage Opress.

## APPRENTICE VS APPRENTICE

When Darth Tyranus begins training Savage Opress, he does not realise that his last student, Asajj Ventress, has actually recruited Opress to destroy him. Torn between two demanding masters, Opress breaks free and attacks them both.

## SITH CLONE

Not every apprentice's apprentice is trained in secret. When Darth Tyranus creates the Force-enhanced clone Jek-14, he proudly presents his new servant to his Master Darth Sidious as the first in an intended army of invincible Sith warriors.

AM I THE ONLY ONE HERE WHO HASN'T BROKEN THE RULE OF TWO YET?!

## SECRET APPRENTICE

When Darth Vader trains a secret apprentice named Starkiller to help him slay the Emperor, Darth Sidious is fully aware of his apprentice's apparent disloyalty. In fact, his intended plan is to have Starkiller replace Vader as his next Sith apprentice!

# WEAPONS OF THE GALAXY

**WHEN TWO HUGE** armies fight for control of the galaxy, it's good to be the guy who's in charge of both sides. Darth Sidious is pleased to see the Republic and the Separatists building up their stores of weaponry. He knows that when the Clone Wars are over, all of it will belong to him.

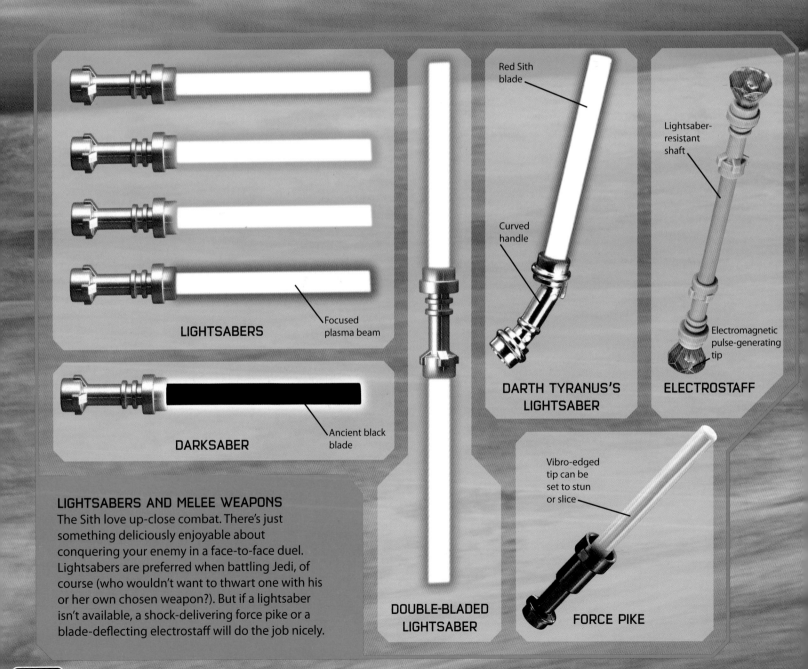

**LIGHTSABERS**

Focused plasma beam

Red Sith blade

Curved handle

**DARTH TYRANUS'S LIGHTSABER**

Lightsaber-resistant shaft

Electromagnetic pulse-generating tip

**ELECTROSTAFF**

**DARKSABER**

Ancient black blade

Vibro-edged tip can be set to stun or slice

**DOUBLE-BLADED LIGHTSABER**

**FORCE PIKE**

## LIGHTSABERS AND MELEE WEAPONS

The Sith love up-close combat. There's just something deliciously enjoyable about conquering your enemy in a face-to-face duel. Lightsabers are preferred when battling Jedi, of course (who wouldn't want to thwart one with his or her own chosen weapon?). But if a lightsaber isn't available, a shock-delivering force pike or a blade-deflecting electrostaff will do the job nicely.

## BLASTERS

Designed to fire energy bolts, blasters come in all shapes and sizes. These weapons may lack the elegance of a lightsaber, but the Sith know the benefits of being able to strike their enemy from afar, and will not hesitate to use any weapon they come across during a battle.

DC-15 BLASTER RIFLE

GEONOSIAN SONIC BLASTER

BLASTER PISTOL

HEAVY BLASTER

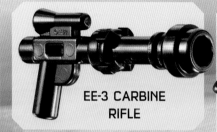

EE-3 CARBINE RIFLE

WOOKIEE BOWCASTER

STANDARD BLASTER

STANDARD BLASTER RIFLE

WOOKIEE BLUNDERBUSS

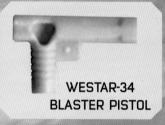

WESTAR-34 BLASTER PISTOL

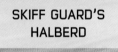

SKIFF GUARD'S HALBERD

RANCOR PROD

EWOK SPEAR

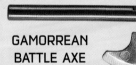

GAMORREAN BATTLE AXE

## PRIMITIVE WEAPONS

Not every weapon runs on electricity. Clubs, spears, axes and bows seem crude at first glance, but all well-trained Sith should be able to turn any object they find into a useful tool of destruction.

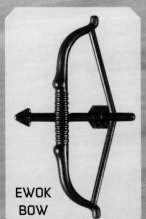

EWOK BOW

## MISSILES AND BOMBS

Explosions can destroy your enemies' equipment, distract them from your true mission or cover your hasty getaway. Sith warriors familiarise themselves with all of the galaxy's demolition devices so that they know what to use – and what to avoid.

GUNGAN ENERGY SPHERE

PROTON TORPEDO

THERMAL DETONATOR

GEONOSIAN MISSILE

# WHAT HAPPENS WHEN A JEDI GIVES IN TO ANGER?

**THE DARK SIDE** is so powerful that even the strongest of Jedi Knights may have to work hard to evade its temptation. Jedi must learn to avoid negative feelings such as fear, anger and hate – or they may be pulled towards the dark side of the Force. What will happen when Anakin Skywalker, who has always had trouble controlling his emotions, gives in to his anger?

Darth **Tyranus** might have been in on Palpatine's kidnap **scheme**, but he certainly wasn't aware of what his **Sith Master** had planned for the finale.

### THE CAPTURED CHANCELLOR
Chancellor Palpatine is an excellent actor. He conceals his true Sith identity even from his closest allies. Palpatine fakes his own kidnapping, luring Anakin and Obi-Wan Kenobi to rescue him. When the Jedi finally track Palpatine down, he is imprisoned by Count Dooku, otherwise known as Darth Tyranus.

## A DEADLY DUEL

Tyranus's dark side powers make him a lethal opponent, and the Sith Lord takes on both Jedi at once. Sensing Anakin's rage and fear, Tyranus taunts him for not using those emotions to fight. Instead of focusing on the light side of the Force, Anakin begins to draw on his anger.

## TYRANUS'S DOWNFALL

The dark side of the Force feeds on anger and hatred. As Anakin duels with increasing rage, he grows more and more powerful. Darth Tyranus underestimates him, and loses more than just his lightsaber. From the sidelines, Chancellor Palpatine orders Anakin to destroy Tyranus. Anakin knows that a good Jedi would not give in to his rage, but he obeys the Chancellor… which is exactly what the devious Sith had planned all along.

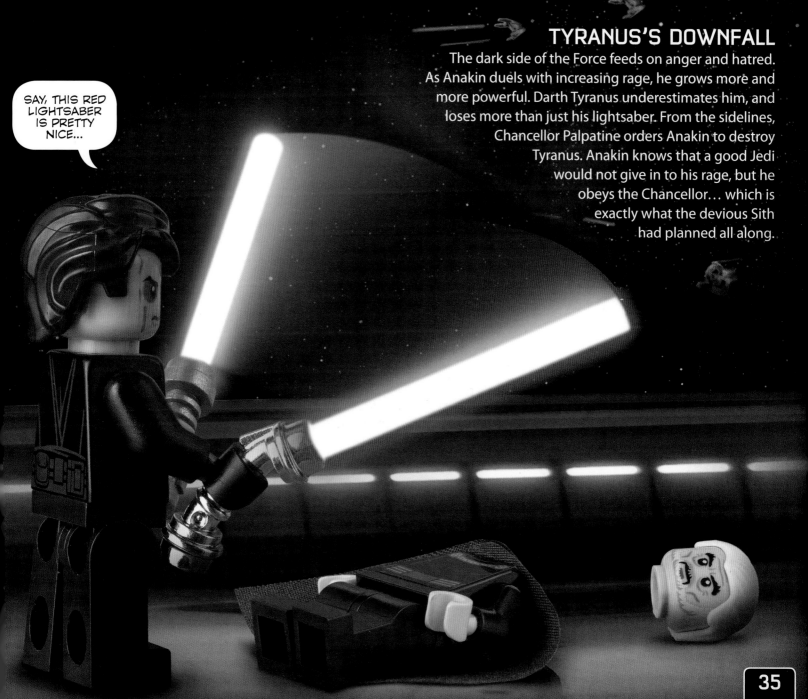

SAY, THIS RED LIGHTSABER IS PRETTY NICE…

# WORKING WITH THE SITH

**IF YOU WANT** your secret plot to take over the galaxy to succeed, you're going to need some outside help. Here are a few of the scoundrels, crooks, bullies and ne'er-do-wells who assist the Sith in achieving their goals. But how to dispose of them when the job is done?

> EVERYBODY RESPECTS A BUG WITH A BEARD.

## POGGLE THE LESSER

The Archduke of Geonosis is one of the leaders of the Separatists. He provides Darth Sidious with the blueprints for his ultimate weapon of galactic supremacy: the Death Star.

### FATE
**Executed by Darth Vader on the Emperor's orders.**

Death Star plans

Beard-like growths

Ornate markings of high rank

Neimoidian warrior

Fancy hat

> I'LL JUST HIDE BACK HERE DURING ALL OF THE ACTION, OKAY?

Expensive robes

## TRADE FEDERATION

This greedy Neimoidian organisation puts Darth Sidious's plan into action by blockading the planet Naboo and helping Palpatine become Chancellor. Nute Gunray is the cowardly viceroy who blindly follows the Sith's instructions

### FATE
**Taken over and eventually dissolved by the Empire.**

## GEONOSIANS

This insect-like species lives in underground hives on the planet Geonosis. Their factories produce endless waves of battle droids for the Separatists. This keeps the Clone Wars going and the Jedi distracted.

**I SMELL A PICNIC AROUND HERE SOMEWHERE!**

Wings indicate warrior status

Armoured exoskeleton

Sonic blaster

### FATE
**Enslaved by the Empire and used for construction labour.**

## GENERAL GRIEVOUS

This Kaleesh warlord envied the power of the Jedi and, following an accident, had almost all of his body replaced with cybernetic parts so he could fight them. He leads the Separatist Droid Army in its attacks against the Republic.

### FATE
**Destroyed by Obi-Wan at the end of the Clone Wars.**

Duranium alloy mask

**I MAY HANG OUT WITH DROIDS, BUT DON'T EVER CONFUSE ME WITH ONE!**

Lightsaber stolen from Jedi victim

Electrostaff

MagnaGuard droid bodyguard

Jabba's second-in-command, Bib Fortuna

**BOS DA WE BARGON! ***

*** TRANSLATION: LET'S MAKE A DEAL!**

Tough – but stupid – Gamorrean guard

## JABBA THE HUTT

The slug-like crime lord and his henchmen are sometimes useful allies to the Sith. They have no problem changing sides, however, if it will be of benefit – and profit – to work with the Jedi instead.

### FATE
**Some bad guys are too big for even the Sith to mess with.**

# ORDER 66

**ALL IS AS DARTH** Sidious has planned. The Jedi Knights are scattered across the galaxy fighting in the Clone Wars, and Anakin Skywalker has sworn allegiance to the Sith as Darth Vader. Sidious sends a message to all the clone commanders: execute Order 66 – the Jedi are traitors and must be destroyed!

## UTAPAU

On the sinkhole planet Utapau, Obi-Wan Kenobi has just defeated the dreaded General Grievous when he is attacked by his own clone troopers under Commander Cody. Unlike most of the Jedi, Obi-Wan manages to escape the ambush.

I SENSE... DANGER!

## SALEUCAMI

On Saleucami, Jedi Master Stass Allie is patrolling on her speeder bike with the loyal Commander Neyo. But when Neyo receives Order 66 from Darth Sidious, he turns his BARC speeder's lasers on his Jedi General.

THERE ARE BAD GUYS AROUND HERE SOMEWHERE...

EXECUTE ORDER 66.

## FELUCIA
As she searches for enemy battle droids on the fungus-covered world of Felucia, Jedi Master Aayla Secura is struck down by the blasters of Clone Commander Bly and his fellow troopers of the 327th Star Corps.

## JEDI TEMPLE
On Coruscant, Sidious commands Darth Vader to attack the Jedi Temple. Obedient to his new Master, Vader leads the 501st Legion to wipe out all the Jedi inside the Temple. The 501st Legion becomes Vader's personal battalion – and is later renamed "Vader's Fist".

## CATO NEIMOIDIA
Jedi Master Plo Koon flies above the Separatist world of Cato Neimoidia in his Jedi starfighter. Although he is a skilled pilot, he is unprepared for his own squadron of ARC-170 starfighters to open fire on his ship from behind.

# WHO WILL WIN: MASTER OR APPRENTICE?

**FOR YEARS, ANAKIN SKYWALKER** has studied the Jedi way under Obi-Wan Kenobi's expert guidance. But now he has fallen to the dark side and become a Sith. Will the newly renamed Darth Vader be strong enough to defeat and destroy his former friend and mentor?

THE JEDI ARE THE REAL BAD GUYS!

HAVE YOU LOOKED IN A MIRROR LATELY?

Lava skiff

## MUSTAFAR CLASH
The volcanic world of Mustafar is a fiery, dangerous place. Obi-Wan follows Vader here to convince his former student to return to the side of good. But Vader's anger against the Jedi Order is far too great – and he declares Obi-Wan to be his enemy. Obi-Wan is left with no choice but to fight his old friend.

Like others who wield the **dark side** of the **Force**, Darth Vader's **hatred** and hunger for power cause his **eyes** to change to yellow and red.

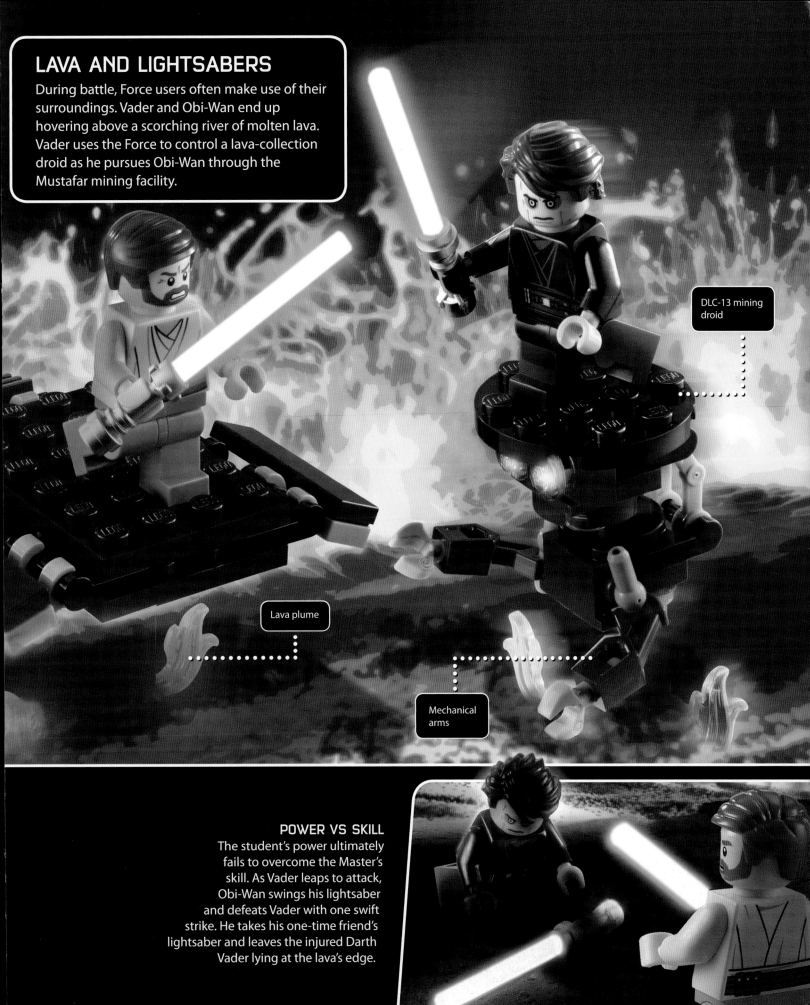

## LAVA AND LIGHTSABERS

During battle, Force users often make use of their surroundings. Vader and Obi-Wan end up hovering above a scorching river of molten lava. Vader uses the Force to control a lava-collection droid as he pursues Obi-Wan through the Mustafar mining facility.

DLC-13 mining droid

Lava plume

Mechanical arms

### POWER VS SKILL

The student's power ultimately fails to overcome the Master's skill. As Vader leaps to attack, Obi-Wan swings his lightsaber and defeats Vader with one swift strike. He takes his one-time friend's lightsaber and leaves the injured Darth Vader lying at the lava's edge.

# CAN A SITH LORD DEFEAT YODA?

**DARTH SIDIOUS COMMANDS** the dark side with such power that he fills his enemies with fear. But can this mightiest of Sith Lords defeat the Grand Master of the Jedi Order? Darth Sidious is eager to find out when Yoda challenges him to an incredible duel in the heart of the Senate building.

Despite all of his **Force** strength, even **wise** Yoda does not sense that Chancellor **Palpatine** is a Sith Lord – until it is **too late!**

### THE NEW EMPEROR
Darth Sidious has transformed the Republic into an Empire! Yoda must take action, and fast, if he is to end the newly crowned Emperor's evil reign. Entering the Senate on Coruscant, Yoda finds his way blocked by the Emperor's Royal Guards. Wasting no time, Yoda effortlessly tosses them aside with the Force.

### BLASTS OF POWER
Sidious deploys Force lightning with deadly skill. He sends a bolt of the crackling energy at Yoda, which hurls the tiny Jedi across the room. Yoda is stunned, but responds with a Force push of his own that sends the Emperor flying. When Sidious tries to get away, Yoda pulls out his lightsaber and challenges the Sith Lord to prove the dark side's power.

YOUR MATCH YOU HAVE FINALLY MET, SIDIOUS.

WE SHALL SEE, MY LITTLE GREEN FRIEND.

## THE SENATE CHAMBER

Sith Lord and Jedi Master do battle atop the former Chancellor's podium. As it rises into the great Senate chamber, it is clear that that Sidious is not a match for Yoda's superior speed and agility. But he has another trick up his black-robed sleeve. With a mad cackle, he uses the Force to lift the chamber's floating Senate pods and throw them at Yoda. Yoda dodges the attack, and returns the favour, sending one pod flying right back at Sidious!

### A MIGHTY FALL

Sidious is an agile Sith and is able to make a quick recovery. He blasts Yoda's lightsaber out of his hand and fires lethal lightning again. Yoda resists it, and the resulting Force explosion flings both fighters backwards. Sidious catches himself, but Yoda plunges to the floor far below. Now it is the injured Jedi's turn to flee. Though his victory is only temporary, the Sith Lord stands triumphant!

# MAN BECOMES MACHINE

**DARTH VADER'S DUEL WITH** Obi-Wan on Mustafar left him badly hurt. In order to save him, Darth Sidious – now Emperor Palpatine – calls on all the technology the Empire has to offer. His medical droids rebuild Vader's burned body with robotic parts, and cover his face with a black mask. He has become more machine than man.

### BATTLE DAMAGE
Searing lava has scarred Vader's face and skin. Although he already had one mechanical arm, Obi-Wan's lightsaber has cost him the other one, along with both legs. Vader cannot even breathe on his own. Will his Master, Emperor Palpatine, find a way to keep him alive?

Surgical Reconstruction Centre

THE SUIT MAY BE A LITTLE ITCHY, BUT YOU CAN'T EVER TAKE IT OFF.

Emperor Palpatine

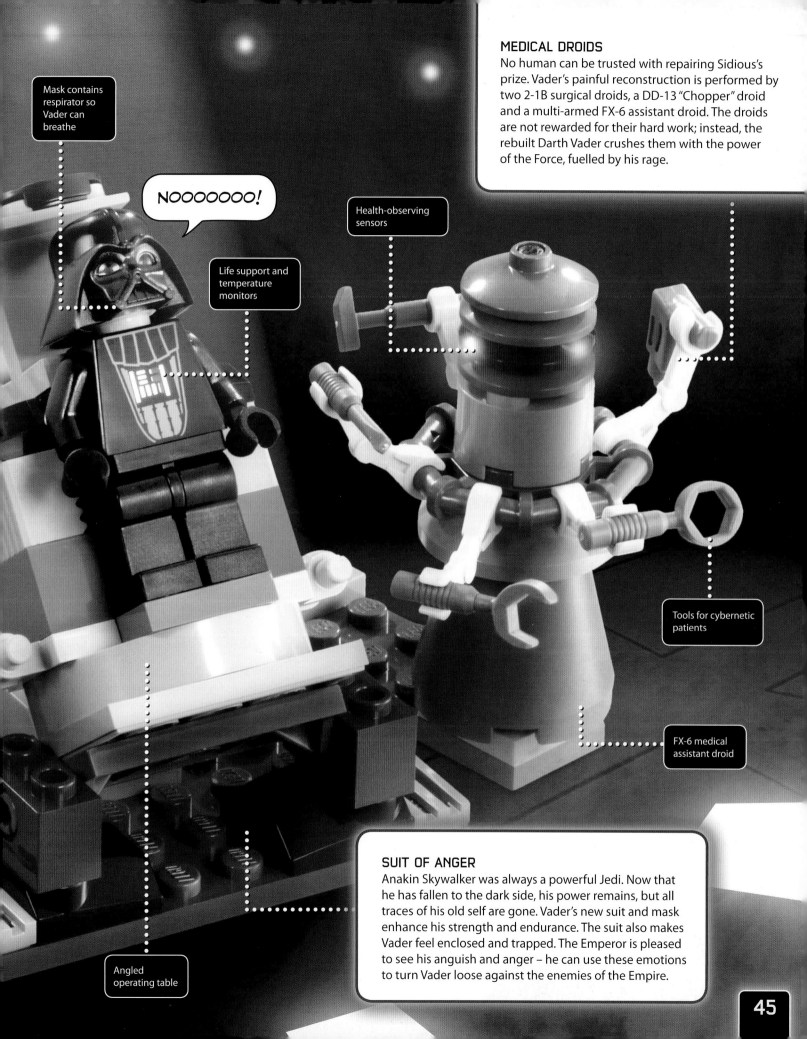

**Mask contains respirator so Vader can breathe**

*NOOOOOOO!*

**Life support and temperature monitors**

## MEDICAL DROIDS
No human can be trusted with repairing Sidious's prize. Vader's painful reconstruction is performed by two 2-1B surgical droids, a DD-13 "Chopper" droid and a multi-armed FX-6 assistant droid. The droids are not rewarded for their hard work; instead, the rebuilt Darth Vader crushes them with the power of the Force, fuelled by his rage.

**Health-observing sensors**

**Tools for cybernetic patients**

**FX-6 medical assistant droid**

**Angled operating table**

## SUIT OF ANGER
Anakin Skywalker was always a powerful Jedi. Now that he has fallen to the dark side, his power remains, but all traces of his old self are gone. Vader's new suit and mask enhance his strength and endurance. The suit also makes Vader feel enclosed and trapped. The Emperor is pleased to see his anguish and anger – he can use these emotions to turn Vader loose against the enemies of the Empire.

**EMPLOYEE OF THE MONTH**
Emperor Palpatine is a very demanding boss. Palpatine once gave Vader a medal for doing a great job… but he soon took it away after Vader accidentally knocked over a battalion of stormtroopers!

Blade powered by crimson crystal

# DARTH VADER

**FEW WHO MEET** him would believe that Darth Vader was once a noble Jedi Knight. He is short-tempered, destructive and cruel, with a strength and rage that are feared by his enemies and allies alike. Even his Imperial underlings avoid him, because to anger Lord Vader is to face doom.

Life support regulation box

Legs replaced with cybernetic limbs

## MILITARY COMMANDER

As the Emperor's military enforcer, Vader commands entire fleets of mighty Star Destroyers in battle. Squadrons of TIE fighters follow his orders, which are most effective when Vader leads in his personal starfighter. His tactical skills make him especially fearsome when hunting fugitive rebels and Jedi.

## DARK LORD

Vader serves as the right-hand man to Emperor Palpatine, who rules the entire Empire of millions of planets and star systems. His duties are to carry out the Emperor's will, enforce the harsh Imperial laws throughout the galaxy and wipe out any Jedi that he can find.

## DATA FILE

- **HOMEWORLD:** TATOOINE
- **BIRTH DATE:** 41 BBY
- **RANK:** SITH LORD
- **TRAINED BY:** OBI-WAN KENOBI, DARTH SIDIOUS
- **WEAPON:** RED-BLADED LIGHTSABER

## "YOU DON'T KNOW THE POWER OF THE DARK SIDE."

DARTH VADER

## THE PATH TO THE DARK SIDE

Anakin Skywalker started out a hero, but his uncontrolled emotions and selfish choices led him to become a Dark Lord of the Sith. His journey to evil was complete when his face and body were sealed inside his black mask and armour.

WOULD YOU USE THE FORCE FOR YOUR OWN GAIN?

**YES**

DO YOU ENJOY OBEYING A MASTER?

# WHAT PATH WILL YOU TAKE?

**NO**

**LIKE MANY OTHER SITH** Lords, Anakin Skywalker started out a hero, but his choices led him down the path to the dark side. How would you end up if you faced the same choices he did? Answer the questions and discover your destiny!

**YES**

DO YOU BREAK THE RULES TO HELP YOUR FRIENDS?

**YES**

**NO**

DO YOU SEEK REVENGE?

**NO**

DO YOU ENJOY THE POWER OF BEING A JEDI KNIGHT?

**NO** — **WOULD YOU DO ANYTHING TO RULE THE GALAXY?** — **YES**

### SITH LORD
You have followed Darth Vader's terrible journey to the dark side and become a powerful Sith Lord. You rule by fear.

**NO**

### FALLEN JEDI
You might once have been a force for good, but the temptation of evil has proven too strong. Like Pong Krell, you are now guided by the dark side.

**YES**

**ARE YOU AFRAID OF FAILURE?** — **YES**

### DARK SIDE WARRIOR
You may not quite have the makings of a full Sith, but you are definitely one of the bad guys. Perhaps you can join Asajj Ventress on her evil adventures.

**NO**

**NO**

### ROGUE
You aren't a shining light of virtue, but you'll still help your friends out when they get in trouble. Jek-14 had to make the choice between dark and light. And so must you!

**NO** — **DO YOU OFTEN DO THE RIGHT THING?**

**YES**

**YES**

### JEDI KNIGHT
You have resisted the lure of the dark side and emerged a brave and noble hero – just like Luke Skywalker. Well done!

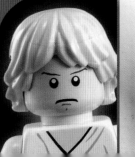

# CHAPTER THREE
# THE EMPIRE ERA

Although the dark side's Empire rules supreme, the forces of good still rise to oppose it. Those who remember the time of the Republic and the Jedi join forces as the Rebel Alliance, and swear to end the Emperor's reign and restore peace and justice to the galaxy.

Darth Sidious cannot allow such insolence. He orders his loyal apprentice Darth Vader to hunt down the rebels and find their hidden bases. And to finish the job, he prepares to use a devastating secret weapon that has been many years in the building…

THE ABILITY TO DESTROY A PLANET IS… ACTUALLY PRETTY IMPRESSIVE, WHEN YOU THINK ABOUT IT.

# THE MAN IN THE MASK

**DARTH VADER'S MASK** and armour cover his entire body. They contain many high-tech mechanisms that keep him alive – and their appearance also intimidates his enemies! Underneath the durasteel plating and padded body suit, cybernetic systems are wired directly into Vader's body, letting him move as if he still had his original limbs.

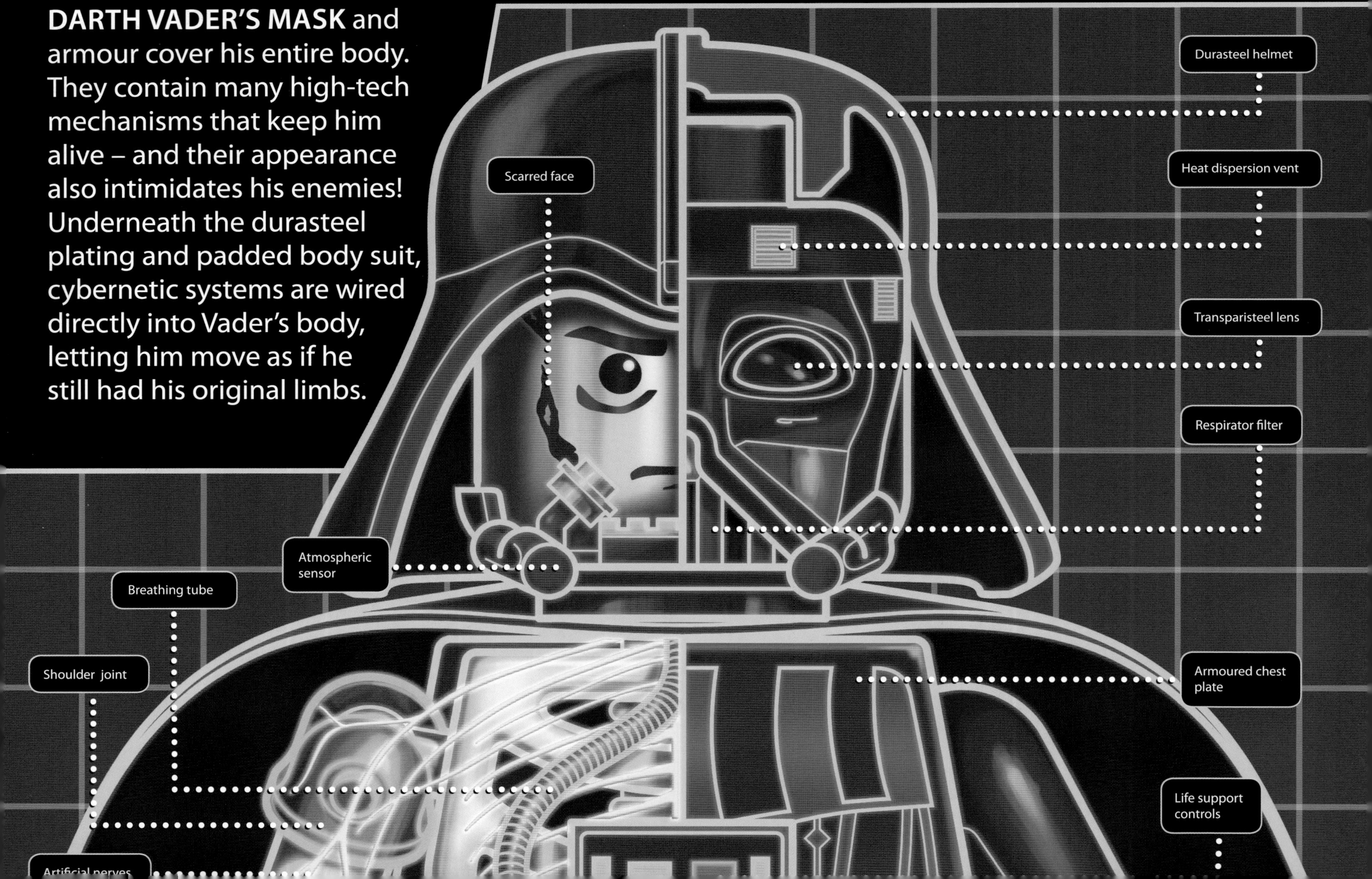

Durasteel helmet

Heat dispersion vent

Transparisteel lens

Respirator filter

Armoured chest plate

Life support controls

Scarred face

Atmospheric sensor

Breathing tube

Shoulder joint

Artificial nerves

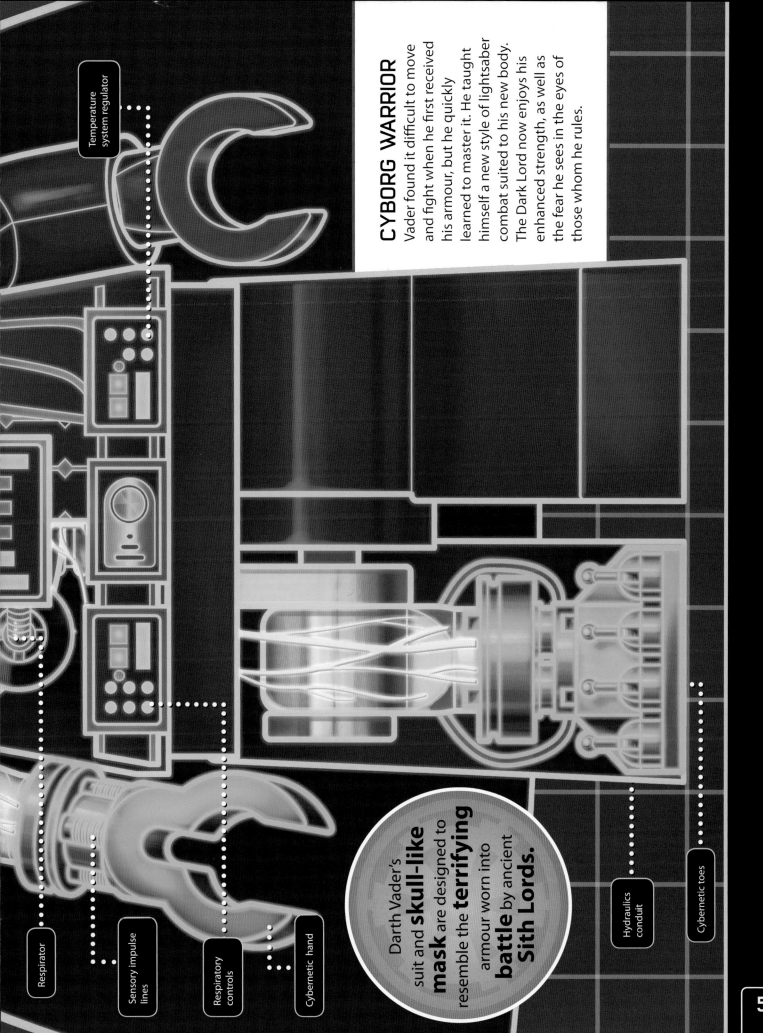

## CYBORG WARRIOR

Vader found it difficult to move and fight when he first received his armour, but he quickly learned to master it. He taught himself a new style of lightsaber combat suited to his new body. The Dark Lord now enjoys his enhanced strength, as well as the fear he sees in the eyes of those whom he rules.

Darth Vader's suit and **skull-like mask** are designed to resemble the **terrifying** armour worn into **battle** by ancient **Sith Lords.**

Temperature system regulator

Respirator

Sensory impulse lines

Respiratory controls

Cybernetic hand

Hydraulics conduit

Cybernetic toes

# BREAKING NEWS

BEEP BLOOP BLEEP!

BREAKING NEWS • DARTH VADER'S IDENTITY FINALLY REVEALED! • SLAVE BOY BECOMES SITH LORD.

**IN A SHOCKING** report, Galaxy News reveals that Darth Vader, one the galaxy's most fearsome villains, is none other than former podracing champion and Jedi hero – Anakin Skywalker. R2-Q2 tracks down a few of Anakin's oldest friends (and foes) to find out what they have to say!

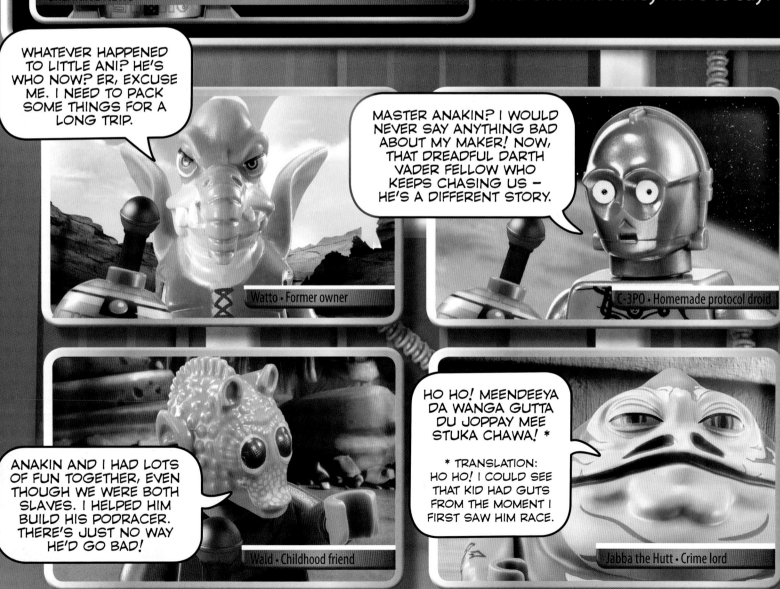

WHATEVER HAPPENED TO LITTLE ANI? HE'S WHO NOW? ER, EXCUSE ME. I NEED TO PACK SOME THINGS FOR A LONG TRIP.

Watto • Former owner

MASTER ANAKIN? I WOULD NEVER SAY ANYTHING BAD ABOUT MY MAKER! NOW, THAT DREADFUL DARTH VADER FELLOW WHO KEEPS CHASING US – HE'S A DIFFERENT STORY.

C-3PO • Homemade protocol droid

ANAKIN AND I HAD LOTS OF FUN TOGETHER, EVEN THOUGH WE WERE BOTH SLAVES. I HELPED HIM BUILD HIS PODRACER. THERE'S JUST NO WAY HE'D GO BAD!

Wald • Childhood friend

HO HO! MEENDEEYA DA WANGA GUTTA DU JOPPAY MEE STUKA CHAWA! *

* TRANSLATION: HO HO! I COULD SEE THAT KID HAD GUTS FROM THE MOMENT I FIRST SAW HIM RACE.

Jabba the Hutt • Crime lord

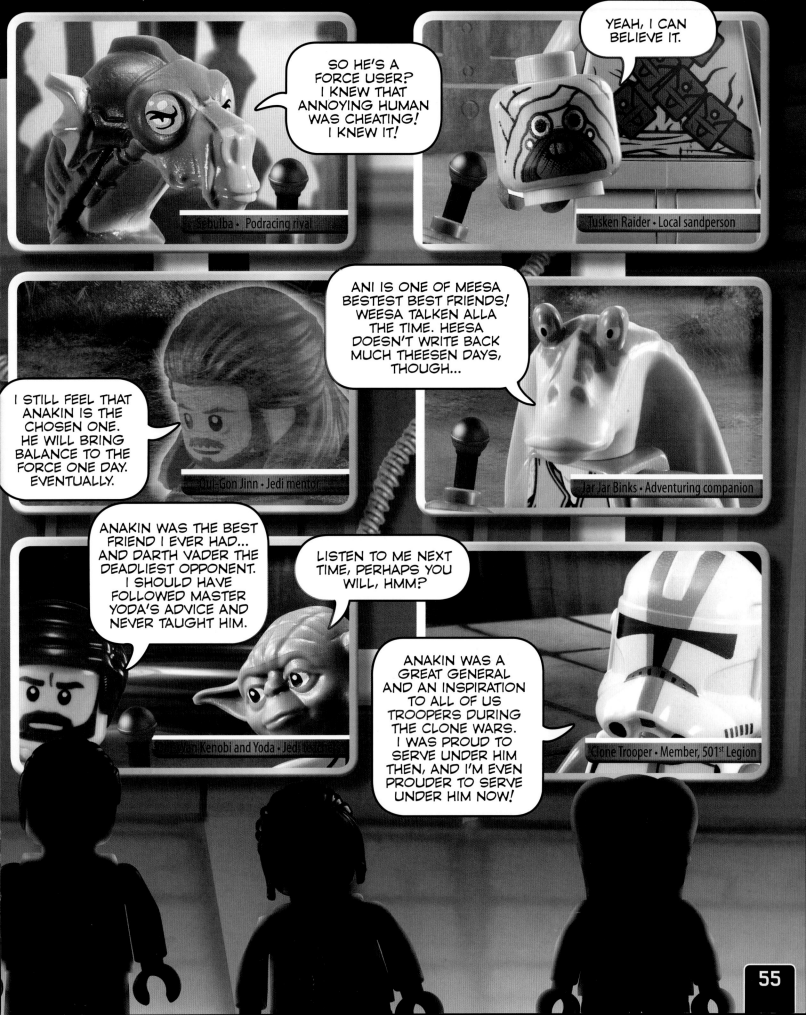

55

# IMPERIAL FORCES

**AFTER MORE THAN 25,000** years, the Republic is no more – long live the Galactic Empire! With Darth Vader as the Emperor's enforcer, the new order rules with an iron fist, crushing any world that dares to resist. A vast army of stormtroopers and technology help the Empire maintain control over the galaxy.

## IMPERIAL INVASION

The Empire believes in overwhelming its enemies through superior numbers and firepower. When Darth Vader discovers a rebel base on the ice planet Hoth, he sends in a squad of mechanised AT-ATs (All Terrain Armoured Transports) to annihilate it.

> BRRR! IT'S A CHILLY JOB, BUT SOMEBODY'S GOT TO DO IT.

> WATCH IT! I'M DRIVING HERE!

## VEHICLES

The vehicle armada of the Empire ranges from massive, space-cruising Star Destroyers to small, one-person speeder bikes that scout and patrol the Empire's remote outposts. In between are walkers, transports and starfighters of all shapes and sizes.

## DATA FILE

- **LEADER:** EMPEROR PALPATINE
- **FOUNDED IN:** 19 BBY
- **MISSION:** TOTAL GALACTIC DOMINATION AND CONTROL

## MILITARY MIGHT

Imperial officers create strategies, win victories and command the Empire's countless legions of stormtroopers – highly trained, elite soldiers in faceless helmets and white plastoid armour. Some Imperial troops wear gear for different environments, such as snowtroopers, who have insulated equipment for cold-weather planets.

There are many other legions of **specialised** Imperial forces, including light-armoured **scout troopers** and lizard-riding **sandtroopers** for desert climates!

STORMTROOPER

Polarising lenses

Utility belt

IMPERIAL OFFICER

SNOWTROOPER

Breather hood

BlasTech E-11 blaster rifle

### THE DEATH STAR
With its planet-destroying superlaser, the first Death Star battle station was built to terrify the galaxy into obeying the Emperor. When it was blown up by the Rebel Alliance, the Empire started work on an even bigger and more powerful version.

## TROOPER EVOLUTION

During the Clone Wars, an army of identical clone troopers fought for the Republic. Over time, their armour was upgraded from Phase I to Phase II style, and finally into the familiar stormtrooper armour of the Empire.

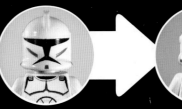

Phase I Clone Trooper

Phase II Clone Trooper

Imperial Stormtrooper

# DARK SIDE TEACHINGS

IN DARTH VADER'S warped vision, the dark side of the Force is all-powerful and the Jedi are traitors who must be destroyed. He believes that peace can come to the galaxy only through an all-controlling leader who cannot be opposed – whether that leader is the Emperor or himself.

"IF YOU'RE NOT WITH ME, THEN YOU'RE MY ENEMY."

"I do not fear the dark side."

"THE EMPEROR IS NOT AS FORGIVING AS I AM."

"The Force is strong with you, young Skywalker, but you are not a Jedi yet."

"ASTEROIDS DO NOT CONCERN ME."

"If you only knew the power of the dark side."

"YOU ARE UNWISE TO LOWER YOUR DEFENCES!"

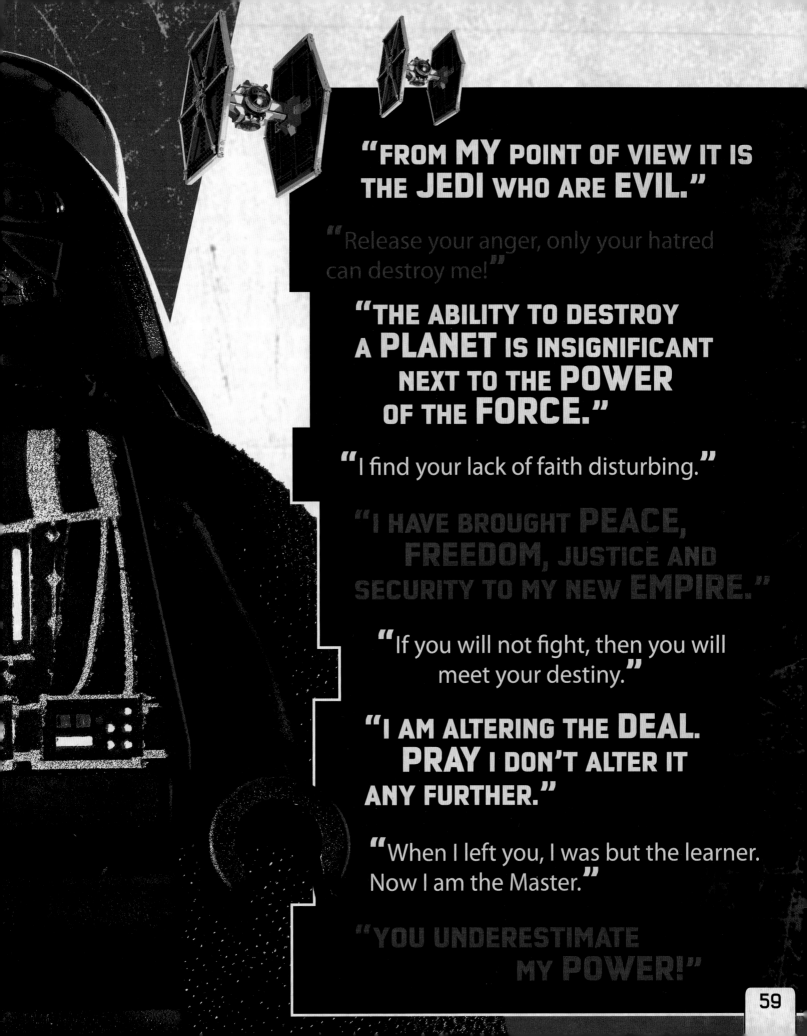

"FROM **MY** POINT OF VIEW IT IS THE **JEDI** WHO ARE **EVIL.**"

"Release your anger, only your hatred can destroy me!"

"**THE ABILITY TO DESTROY A PLANET IS INSIGNIFICANT NEXT TO THE POWER OF THE FORCE.**"

"I find your lack of faith disturbing."

"**I HAVE BROUGHT PEACE, FREEDOM, JUSTICE AND SECURITY TO MY NEW EMPIRE.**"

"If you will not fight, then you will meet your destiny."

"**I AM ALTERING THE DEAL. PRAY I DON'T ALTER IT ANY FURTHER.**"

"When I left you, I was but the learner. Now I am the Master."

"**YOU UNDERESTIMATE MY POWER!**"

# SECRET APPRENTICE

**THERE CAN BE ONLY** two Sith at a time: a Master and an apprentice. But what happens when the apprentice seeks to become the Master? Darth Vader tries to find out by secretly training his own apprentice, whom he codenames Starkiller.

## DATA FILE

- **HOMEWORLD:** KASHYYYK
- **BIRTH DATE:** 19 BBY
- **RANK:** SITH APPRENTICE
- **TRAINED BY:** DARTH VADER
- **WEAPON:** RED-BLADED LIGHTSABER

Clothes tattered in battle

Bandaged injury

Stripped-down lightsaber handle

When his plans for **Starkiller** fail, Darth Vader doesn't **give up** – he just creates a **clone** of Galen Marek and starts all over again!

## STARKILLER

Starkiller is really Galen Marek, the Force-strong son of two Jedi Knights. Darth Vader captures him as a child and raises him to be a dark side assassin in order to help Vader destroy his own Master, Darth Sidious.

# "I AM THE FUTURE OF THE SITH!"
STARKILLER

## ROGUE SHADOW
To help his apprentice on his stealthy missions, Darth Vader gives him a one-of-a-kind starship, *Rogue Shadow*. Its advanced hyperdrive and experimental cloaking device enable Starkiller to fly anywhere in the galaxy undetected.

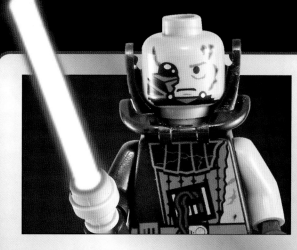

## VADER DEFEATED
Galen Marek remembers his true origins and eventually rejects the way of the Sith. He challenges Vader to a duel, during which his training and knowledge of dark side powers help him overpower his former Master.

Advanced cloaking technology conceals starship

Rotating wings

Laser cannons

Cockpit

## JUNO ECLIPSE
The *Rogue Shadow*'s pilot is Juno Eclipse, a loyal Imperial officer. Over the course of her adventures with Starkiller, she comes to see the evils of the Empire and eventually joins the newly formed Rebel Alliance.

# POWERS OF THE DARK SIDE

**THE DARK SIDE** promises immense knowledge and strength to those who study the ways of the Sith. It also offers special powers, many of which are forbidden to the Jedi. Here are some of the strange and dangerous abilities that Sith Lords can call upon to frighten their followers and vanquish their foes.

*TWICE THE TRAINING, TWICE THE POWER.*

## DOUBLE TROUBLE
Count Dooku had already gained the full skills of a Jedi Master when he joined the dark side and became Darth Tyranus. Now he is twice the threat, using all of the deadly powers at his disposal while he battles opponents with his flashing lightsaber blade.

*YIKES! IT'S GETTING A LITTLE WINDY IN HERE!*

## TELEKINESIS
One of Darth Vader's mightiest talents is the ability to lift objects without touching them, and then throw them through the air at his opponents. Vader uses this power against Luke Skywalker on Cloud City, battering the unsuspecting rebel with metal wreckage and smashing the large protective window behind him.

### FORCE LIGHTNING
By channelling dark side energy through his body, a Sith Lord like Darth Sidious can hurl crackling electricity from his bare hands to punish or destroy those who anger him. Only a great Jedi can hope to resist this shocking power.

Some S? Lords are so i? the **Force**, they when an **enemy** is n? They can use the strength of people's **emotions** to peer into their minds and **read** their feelings!

### LIGHTSABER COMBAT
A Force-sensitive warrior can predict an enemy's moves and block them with his lightsaber, or detect just the right moment to strike. When fighting someone with similar talents, a Sith like Darth Maul also uses savage surprise attacks to win the duel.

YOU'D BETTER BE.

ACK! S-SORRY I F-FORGOT YOUR BIRTHDAY, LORD VADER!

### FORCE CHOKE
A common penalty for failing or displeasing Vader is the Force choke, which even works across large distances. A fortunate victim may be released if the Sith Lord is feeling merciful. As for the less fortunate ones… well, there are always more Imperial officers looking for a promotion.

# REBEL ALLIANCE

**ALL THE EMPEROR** wants is to be the unquestioned and absolute ruler of the galaxy forever, but for some reason those pesky rebels keep interfering. They steal his secret plans, destroy his battle station and make a nuisance of themselves at every turn. Why won't they just leave him alone?!

Traditional Alderaanian hair style

## HEROES OF THE REBELLION

The Rebel Alliance is made up of beings from many worlds, all united by their desire to free the galaxy from Darth Sidious's tyranny. Anyone brave enough can join: from royalty like Princess Leia Organa, to disreputable smugglers like Han Solo.

Practical, casual smuggler's outfit

DL-44 heavy blaster pistol

HAN SOLO

## DATA FILE

 **LEADER:** MON MOTHMA

 **FOUNDED IN:** 2 BBY

 **MISSION:** RESTORE THE GALAXY TO A REPUBLIC

BEEP BOOP BLORP?

NO, ARTOO, I'M NOT SURE WHAT WE'RE REBELLING AGAINST.

## REBEL HELPERS
Droids can be rebels, too. Fearless R2-D2 and always-worried C-3PO join their friends on many important missions. Without them, the Rebellion would not have found Luke Skywalker, blown up the Death Star, beaten Jabba the Hutt or befriended the Ewoks on Endor!

## REBEL COMMAND
The leaders of the Rebellion are always on the run from the dark side's forces. Their hidden bases move from planet to planet and from starship to starship as they try to stay one step ahead of the Empire while thinking up strategies to defeat it.

Death Star II hologram

Rebel leader Mon Mothma

WHAT IF THIS NEW DEATH STAR IS A TRAP?

THEN DESTROYING IT WILL BE A SNAP!

Rebel briefing room aboard the star cruiser *Home One*

AFTER THIS MEETING, I'LL NEED A NAP.

Admiral Ackbar, an amphibious Mon Calamari

DON'T WORRY, WE HAVE A MAP.

General Crix Madine, a former Imperial officer

Newly-promoted general, Lando Calrissian

Ceremonial dress for special occasions

**PRINCESS LEIA**

## REBELS OF LOTHAL
On an Outer Rim planet named Lothal, a group of determined rebels refuse to accept the new Imperial rule. Although they are vastly outnumbered by stormtroopers, Zeb, Ezra and their fellow rebels will do anything they can to take down the Empire.

TAKING OVER THE GALAXY? PIECE OF CAKE!

# GALACTIC DOMINATION

**TO MOST OF ITS** inhabitants, the galaxy is filled with fascinating alien worlds and cultures. But to Emperor Palpatine, every planet is just one more place to conquer in order to expand the Empire. Each planet poses unique opportunities and threats. Where will the Emperor go next?

## ALDERAAN

"This mountainous world claims to be peaceful, but rumour has it that it's chock-full of rebel spies and other anti-Imperial traitors, all the way up to the royal Organa family. Still, Alderaan is a pretty place. It's a shame the planet has become such a threat to my Empire."

**MISSION: Destroy at the earliest opportunity**.

## TATOOINE

"Ugh, Tatooine. Darth Vader tells me such horror stories about that desert planet. Too much sand for me – it's itchy and annoying and gets everywhere. Note to sandtroopers: pack plenty of water and dewback food."

**MISSION: Avoid at all costs**.

## YAVIN 4

"Who lives on a moon? Apparently a bunch of people, because there are old stone pyramids all over the place. The jungles are full of bugs and other creepy-crawlies, so it's a good thing I can scare them off with the Force. Not that I'd ever go there unless it turned out to have a secret rebel base, ha ha."

**MISSION: Keep an eye on Yavin 4 – from a distance.**

## ENDOR

"A forest moon populated by harmless, fuzzy teddy bear creatures. Rumours of sophisticated tree-and-rock booby traps are probably exaggerated. This is an excellent isolated location for building the new Death Star's shield generator where no one will disturb us."

**MISSION: Build generator. Minimal security necessary.**

## HOTH

"Frozen planets like this are why the Empire spends so many credits on cold-weather trooper gear. The ice fields may be slippery, but all-terrain walkers should be able to stomp their way across. If my robes weren't so toasty warm, I'd get chilly just looking at it!"

**MISSION: Easy to conquer. Invade immediately.**

## BESPIN

"A gas giant of interest only to miners and get-rich-quick types. The Cloud City mining outpost that floats above it is of little importance, but might be worth making an example of to ensure nobody else thinks they're beyond the Empire's reach. A detachment of stormtroopers should be sufficient."

**MISSION: Show them who's boss.**

## CORUSCANT

"The Imperial Centre – my official headquarters (when I'm not holidaying on the Death Star). No one threatens the Empire's seat of power, thanks to all of the stormtroopers and Royal Guards stationed here."

**MISSION: Continue with top-level security operation. And keep an eye out for anyone in a brown-hooded robe hanging around the abandoned Jedi Temple.**

# CAN A PRINCESS OUTWIT A SITH LORD?

DARTH VADER HAS faced and defeated many opponents. However, when he captures a royal senator from the planet Alderaan, the mighty Sith Lord may have finally met his match. Will Princess Leia give away the secret location of the Rebel Alliance base, or will she resist her furious captor and keep her friends and allies safe?

Although **Darth Vader** does not realise it, he is actually **questioning** his own daughter! When Leia was born, she was **hidden** from her father on the planet Alderaan.

### DEATH STAR PLANS
The Empire has secretly built an enormous battle station called the Death Star. When Princess Leia steals its blueprints, Darth Vader tracks her down to recover them. Leia hides the plans inside R2-D2 and sends the astromech droid on a mission to find Obi-Wan Kenobi and deliver them to him.

### IMPERIAL INTERROGATOR
Many terrifying droids are at the Empire's disposal. When Leia refuses to answer his questions, Vader brings in a hovering interrogation droid. This infamous droid uses chemicals and medical scanners on stubborn prisoners. Usually, just the sight of this droid is scary enough to make even the bravest prisoner talk.

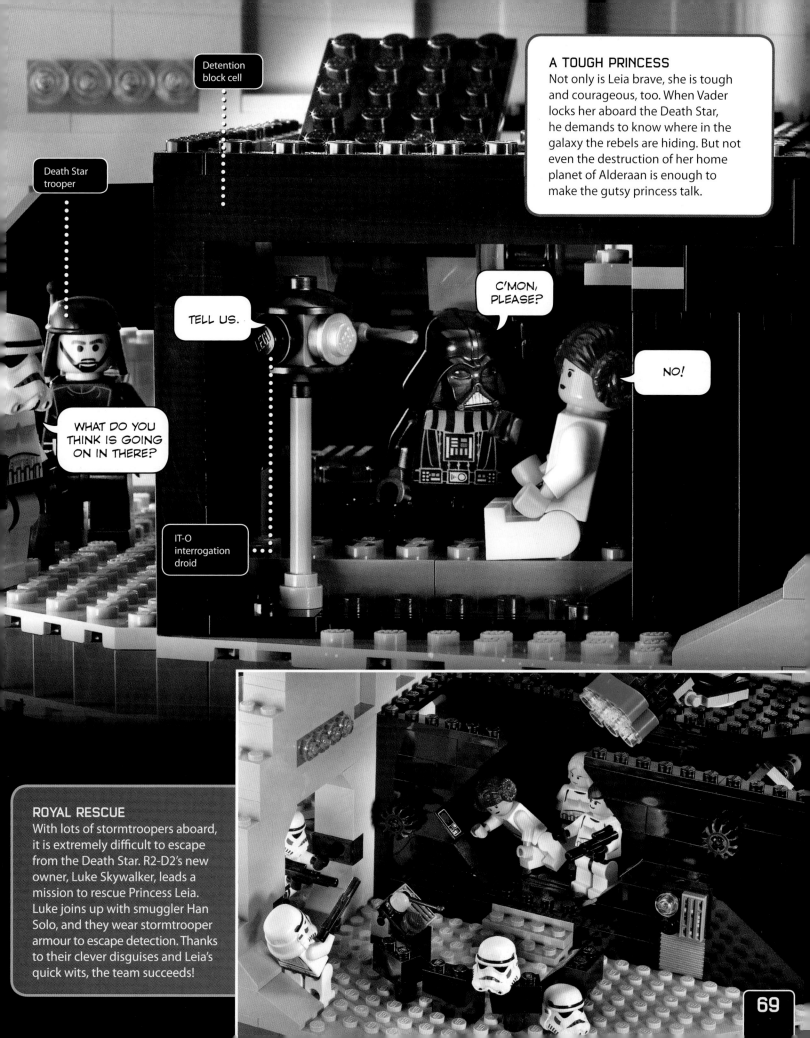

Detention block cell

Death Star trooper

IT-O interrogation droid

TELL US.

WHAT DO YOU THINK IS GOING ON IN THERE?

C'MON, PLEASE?

NO!

## A TOUGH PRINCESS
Not only is Leia brave, she is tough and courageous, too. When Vader locks her aboard the Death Star, he demands to know where in the galaxy the rebels are hiding. But not even the destruction of her home planet of Alderaan is enough to make the gutsy princess talk.

## ROYAL RESCUE
With lots of stormtroopers aboard, it is extremely difficult to escape from the Death Star. R2-D2's new owner, Luke Skywalker, leads a mission to rescue Princess Leia. Luke joins up with smuggler Han Solo, and they wear stormtrooper armour to escape detection. Thanks to their clever disguises and Leia's quick wits, the team succeeds!

# THE DEATH STAR

**HOW DO YOU KEEP** an entire galaxy in line? If you're Darth Sidious, you build a moon-sized battle station capable of blowing up an entire planet with a single blast. Sure, it might be a little extreme, but it's guaranteed to stop the citizens of your Empire from complaining all the time!

The Death Star took about **20 years** to build… and about **20 minutes** for rebel pilot Luke Skywalker to **destroy!**

### THRONE ROOM
Wherever he goes, the Emperor always wants to be in control. All of his palaces, command ships and even the Death Star itself are equipped with throne rooms from where he can give orders and watch over his Empire.

### TIE FIGHTER HANGARS
Just in case any troublesome rebels come calling, the Death Star's hangars hold about 7,000 TIE fighters ready for battle. When needed, these ships drop down from ceiling-mounted storage racks and launch out into space.

### BRIDGE SHAFT
The Death Star is not entirely pedestrian-friendly. It is full of deep shafts and chasms, with only narrow retracting bridges to let its occupants cross. If a bridge fails to deploy, then good luck – better hope you have a grappling hook on you!

## DEATH STAR 1
The original Death Star is 120 km (75 miles) across, with a disc-shaped focusing lens for its devastatingly powerful superlaser. The Emperor thinks it is indestructible, but a tiny thermal exhaust port proves to be its one weakness.

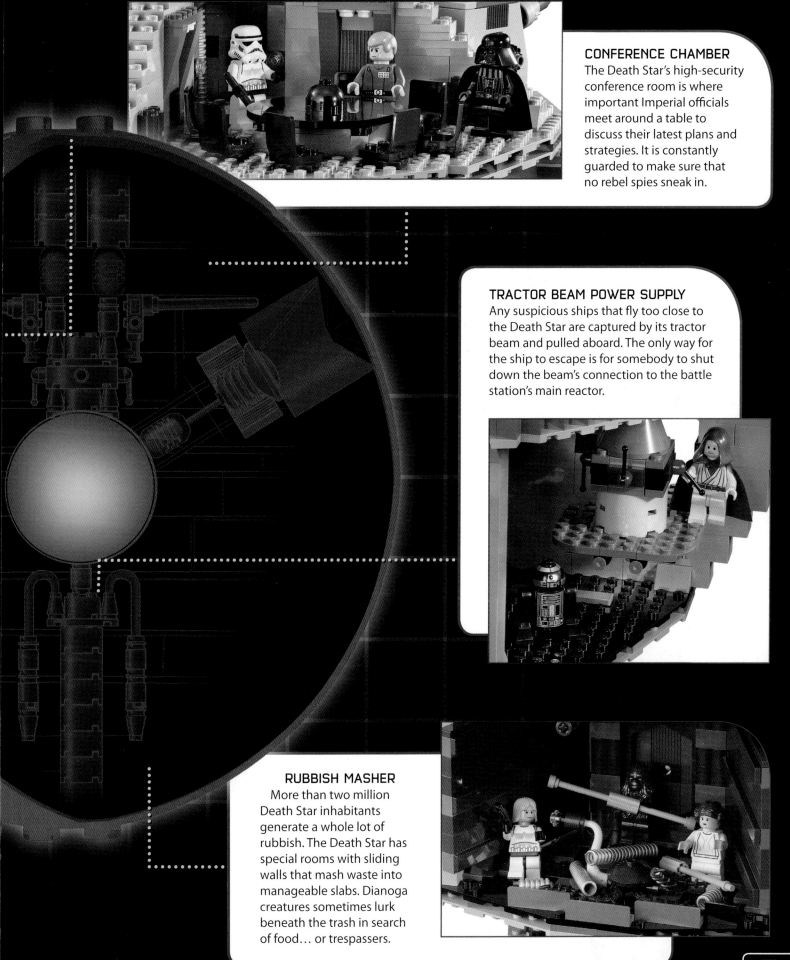

## CONFERENCE CHAMBER
The Death Star's high-security conference room is where important Imperial officials meet around a table to discuss their latest plans and strategies. It is constantly guarded to make sure that no rebel spies sneak in.

## TRACTOR BEAM POWER SUPPLY
Any suspicious ships that fly too close to the Death Star are captured by its tractor beam and pulled aboard. The only way for the ship to escape is for somebody to shut down the beam's connection to the battle station's main reactor.

## RUBBISH MASHER
More than two million Death Star inhabitants generate a whole lot of rubbish. The Death Star has special rooms with sliding walls that mash waste into manageable slabs. Dianoga creatures sometimes lurk beneath the trash in search of food… or trespassers.

# OBI-WAN KENOBI

**ONCE, OBI-WAN KENOBI** was Anakin Skywalker's teacher and best friend, but that ended when Anakin became Darth Vader. Obi-Wan went into hiding after the Jedi were defeated, and Vader has never been able to find him. When they meet again on the Death Star, Vader finally has his chance for revenge.

**Darth Vader** never guessed that his enemy **Obi-Wan** was living on Anakin Skywalker's own **home planet** of **Tatooine!**

Hangar bay entrance

*Millennium Falcon* in hangar bay

I HAVE THE STRANGEST SENSE OF DÉJÀ VU.

YOU TOO?

Retracted blast door

## DEATH STAR DUEL

Vader senses Obi-Wan's presence aboard the Empire's secret battle station and confronts him. They duel with lightsabers, but Obi-Wan disappears as Vader strikes the finishing blow, becoming one with the Force.

" **IF YOU STRIKE ME DOWN, I SHALL BECOME MORE POWERFUL THAN YOU CAN POSSIBLY IMAGINE.** "

OBI-WAN KENOBI

## FORMER ALLIES

Obi-Wan has known Anakin Skywalker since Anakin was very young. As Jedi partners, they shared many adventures. Obi-Wan always knew that Anakin was reckless and overconfident, but he never dreamed that his apprentice might fall to the dark side.

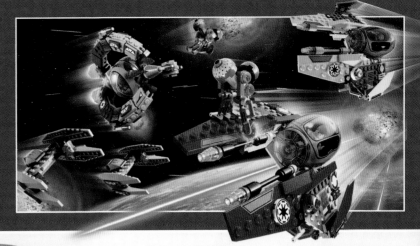

Grey hair

Old Jedi robes double as hermit disguise

Rarely used lightsaber

## ON VACATION

Obi-Wan was one of the hardest-working Jedi Knights, but his life wasn't all fighting Sith, foiling Separatist plots and instructing his rebellious Padawan. Between missions, Obi-Wan liked to kick back and relax by the pool on the peaceful planet Alderaan.

## LIFE IN EXILE

As one of the few Jedi to survive the Clone Wars, Obi-Wan fled to Tatooine. Disguised as a desert hermit known as "Old Ben" Kenobi, he has spent the years watching over Anakin's son, Luke, waiting for the day when he can train the boy in the Force.

## DATA FILE

- **HOMEWORLD:** STEWJON
- **BIRTH DATE:** 57 BBY
- **RANK:** JEDI MASTER
- **TRAINED BY:** QUI-GON JINN
- **WEAPON:** BLUE-BLADED LIGHTSABER

# WHY IS DARTH VADER'S TIE FIGHTER SPECIAL?

**THERE ARE THOUSANDS** of TIE starfighters in the Empire's armada, but one stands out from all the rest. Darth Vader's prototype TIE Advanced x1 is tougher, faster and cooler-looking than any normal TIE fighter – and unlike its mass-produced brethren, it is far from disposable.

THE ONLY PROBLEM IS ALL THE SPACE-BUGS ON THE WINDSCREEN!

## DEATH STAR BATTLE

When rebels attack the first Death Star, Darth Vader decides to handle things personally. Leading a team of TIE fighters, he flies his TIE/x1 into battle and quickly destroys most of the remaining rebel X-wings and Y-wings. Even though his ship is damaged in the fight, its enhanced armour and shields keep Vader alive… if a bit dizzy!

L-s9.3 laser cannon

Signature bent-wing design

Some of the TIE Advanced x1's **upgrades** can be seen in later Imperial fighters, including the **TIE Interceptor** and the less common **TIE Bomber.**

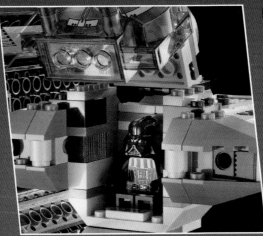

## INSIDE THE X1

Although the TIE Advanced is larger than a standard-issue TIE fighter, there is still only room for a single pilot in the cockpit. Like other TIE fighters, the x1 lacks a life-support system, so Vader must rely on his Force-enhanced flight skills to keep him safe in battle. The x1 has an improved computer tracking system, which helps its lasers lock onto fast-moving enemy ships – and fire on target.

## HYPERDRIVE

Other TIE fighters have to stay close to their Imperial carriers and bases, but not this one! Unlike those short-range ships, the TIE/x1 has a Class 4.0 hyperdrive built into its extended back section that lets it move between star systems faster than the speed of light. This gives Vader great freedom to travel… though only where the Emperor permits him to go.

## DEFLECTOR SHIELD

A standard TIE fighter has no deflector shield, so it explodes after taking just one or two hits from an enemy's laser cannons. Darth Vader's vessel is covered with a durasteel alloy that resists blaster fire. If that isn't enough, the x1 is also protected by a deflector shield – a force field that draws power from the ship's solar ionization reactor to block laser bolts and space debris.

Solar energy collector panel

# LUKE SKYWALKER

**ANAKIN SKYWALKER'S SON,** Luke, is hidden from his father on Tatooine, where he grows up as a farm boy far from the reach of the Empire and the dark side. When he is drawn into the galactic conflict, Luke joins forces with the rebels. He must quickly learn to be a Jedi… before he faces Darth Vader himself!

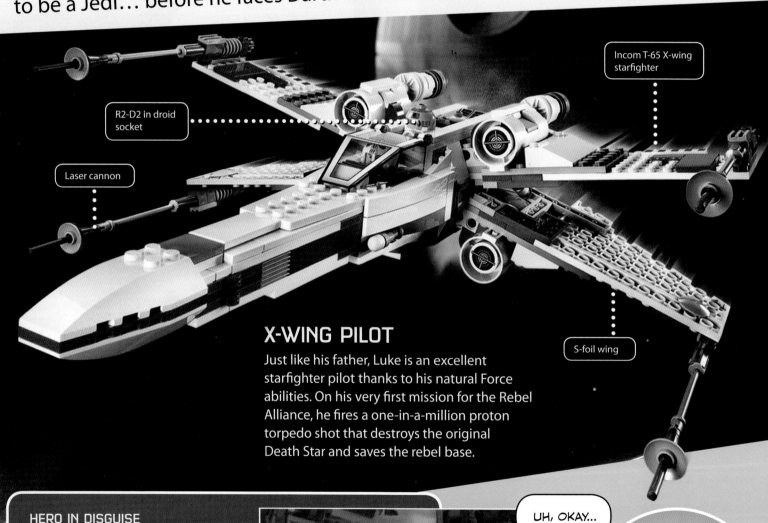

R2-D2 in droid socket

Incom T-65 X-wing starfighter

Laser cannon

S-foil wing

## X-WING PILOT

Just like his father, Luke is an excellent starfighter pilot thanks to his natural Force abilities. On his very first mission for the Rebel Alliance, he fires a one-in-a-million proton torpedo shot that destroys the original Death Star and saves the rebel base.

## HERO IN DISGUISE
Obi-Wan and Yoda always feared that Luke might follow in Anakin's footsteps, but this isn't what they had in mind! Chased by his fans, Luke puts on a cheap Darth Vader costume and somehow ends up in command of a squad of Imperial troops.

UH, OKAY...

NOW BLOW UP YOUR OWN BARRACKS!

Obi-Wan didn't tell **Luke** much about his father. All Luke knew was that **Anakin Skywalker** was a great Jedi Knight… and that he had been destroyed by **Darth Vader!**

**Green-bladed lightsaber**

## A DARK WARNING

As part of Luke's Jedi training, his Master, Yoda, sends him into a cave that is strong with the dark side. Inside, Luke faces a vision of Darth Vader that transforms into Luke himself – a sign of what could be his own destiny… if he isn't careful.

**Glove covers robotic hand**

## MONSTER BATTLE

Luke's Jedi training has equipped him with quick wits and even faster reflexes. When he comes face to face with Jabba the Hutt's rancor beast, Luke has to act fast. He wedges a large bone into the rancor's mouth, giving himself time to escape.

## DATA FILE

-  **HOMEWORLD:** TATOOINE
-  **BIRTH DATE:** 19 BBY
-  **RANK:** JEDI KNIGHT
-  **TAUGHT BY:** OBI-WAN KENOBI, YODA
-  **WEAPON:** BLUE- AND LATER GREEN-BLADED LIGHTSABER

## SITH OR JEDI?

Luke's headstrong nature and natural Force powers make him a perfect candidate for a new Sith apprentice. Darth Sidious wants to recruit him to replace Darth Vader, but Luke is determined to bring Vader back to the side of good instead.

> **"I AM A JEDI, LIKE MY FATHER BEFORE ME."**
>
> LUKE SKYWALKER

**Black fighting clothes**

# DARTH VADER: FAMILY MAN?

It's me, with my shiny new medal!

**TAKE A PEEK INSIDE** Darth Vader's extended family album. Learn about everyone from his secret bride to his rebellious kids – plus a few others who have had an influence on his life along the way!

DARTH VADER IS NUMBER 1

Do this, do that! Don't get angry. Blah blah blah!

Obi-DUMB Kenobi has a bad feeling about this.

## OBI-WAN KENOBI

The big brother I never had... or wanted. A goody-two-shoes perfect Jedi, always telling me what to do. He's just jealous that I'm so strong in the Force!

## QUI-GON JINN

If I had a father, I'd want him to be like Qui-Gon. He was nice and clever and said I would bring balance to the Force. Guess he was wrong!

"You're special, Ani!"

My top weapon ideas:

Death Triangle →

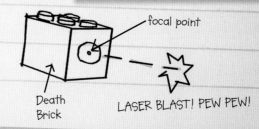
focal point

Death Brick

LASER BLAST! PEW PEW!

# R2-D2 AND C-3PO

I built Threepio all by myself and put lots of gadgets into Artoo. Maybe that makes them like my wacky nephews. Wonder what they're up to these days?

Don't get sand in those joints, guys! Don't steal my secret plans, either.

# PADMÉ AMIDALA

The girl of my dreams. I always knew we'd get married someday. Things would be a lot different if she were still here...

XOXO 4-EVA

# LUKE SKYWALKER

So it turns out I have a son! My boss wants me to get him to join the family business. Maybe he'd like an awesome robot hand just like his Dad has!

Stop breaking Daddy's toys, kid.

Death Star

BANG!

X-wing

# LEIA ORGANA

This rebel princess is always messing up my plans. Is it just me, or does she look a little like Padmé? Could she be...? Naah, no way.

Stay away from smugglers! You don't know where they've been.

# THE HOLOCRON HUNT

**THE JEDI HOLOCRONS** are a source of great power because they contain the entire history of Jedi knowledge. After Order 66, Yoda and Obi-Wan Kenobi (with help from Jek-14) decided to hide the Holocrons from the Sith, so they buried them on Tatooine. Now Luke Skywalker wants to use them to complete his Jedi training… but Darth Vader senses the Holocrons, too, and the race is on!

Magnetic suction tube

UTINNI!

Glowing eyes

### A FAMILIAR RIDE
In order to cross Tatooine's deadly Dune Sea, Luke borrows a speedy podracer. Although it is old and from a local junk shop, the podracer is perfect for manoeuvring across the harsh desert surface – thanks to the triple yellow air scoops on each engine. As Luke zooms along, little does he suspect that he is driving the very same racer that his father Anakin built and used to win his freedom from slavery many years before.

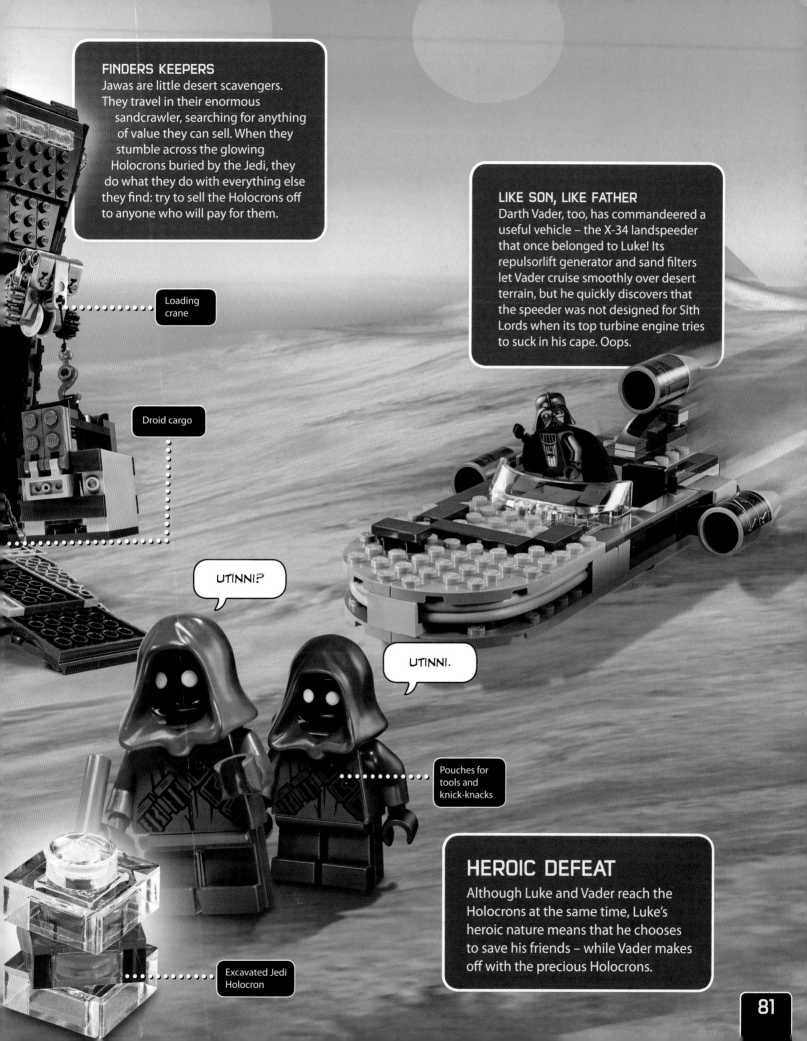

**FINDERS KEEPERS**
Jawas are little desert scavengers. They travel in their enormous sandcrawler, searching for anything of value they can sell. When they stumble across the glowing Holocrons buried by the Jedi, they do what they do with everything else they find: try to sell the Holocrons off to anyone who will pay for them.

**LIKE SON, LIKE FATHER**
Darth Vader, too, has commandeered a useful vehicle – the X-34 landspeeder that once belonged to Luke! Its repulsorlift generator and sand filters let Vader cruise smoothly over desert terrain, but he quickly discovers that the speeder was not designed for Sith Lords when its top turbine engine tries to suck in his cape. Oops.

Loading crane

Droid cargo

UTINNI?

UTINNI.

Pouches for tools and knick-knacks

**HEROIC DEFEAT**
Although Luke and Vader reach the Holocrons at the same time, Luke's heroic nature means that he chooses to save his friends – while Vader makes off with the precious Holocrons.

Excavated Jedi Holocron

# BOUNTY HUNTERS

**SO, REBELS HAVE** blown up your top-secret planet-destroying space station, and the pilot who did it is the son you never knew you had. He's on the run somewhere in the galaxy, but how will you find him? If you're Darth Vader, you just hire a bounty hunter. In fact, you hire a bunch of them!

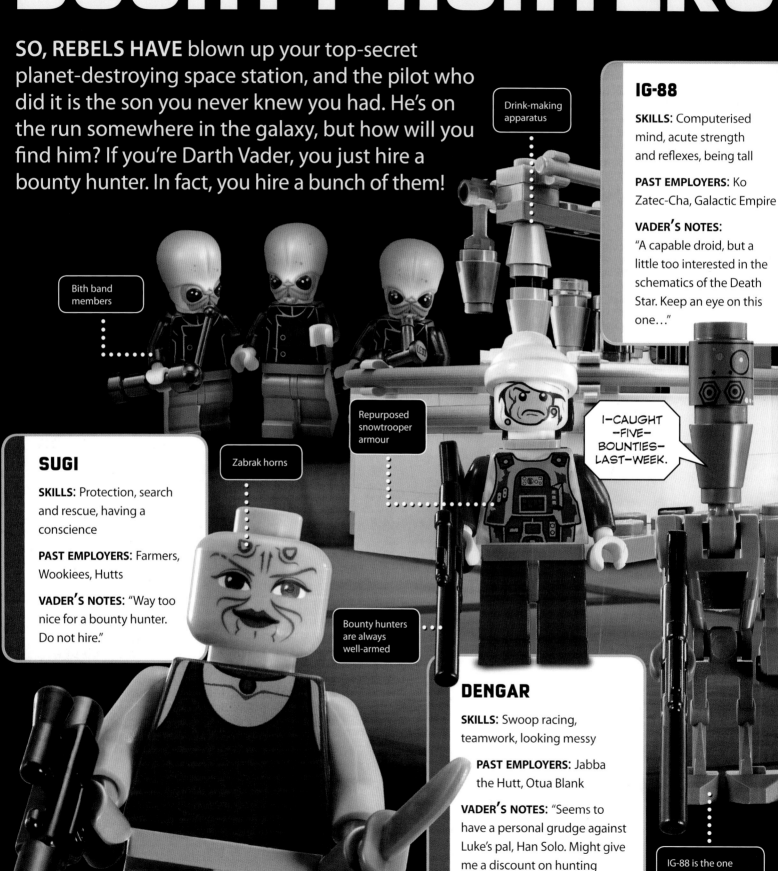

Drink-making apparatus

Bith band members

Zabrak horns

Repurposed snowtrooper armour

Bounty hunters are always well-armed

I–CAUGHT –FIVE– BOUNTIES– LAST–WEEK.

## IG-88

**SKILLS:** Computerised mind, acute strength and reflexes, being tall

**PAST EMPLOYERS:** Ko Zatec-Cha, Galactic Empire

**VADER'S NOTES:** "A capable droid, but a little too interested in the schematics of the Death Star. Keep an eye on this one…"

## SUGI

**SKILLS:** Protection, search and rescue, having a conscience

**PAST EMPLOYERS:** Farmers, Wookiees, Hutts

**VADER'S NOTES:** "Way too nice for a bounty hunter. Do not hire."

## DENGAR

**SKILLS:** Swoop racing, teamwork, looking messy

**PAST EMPLOYERS:** Jabba the Hutt, Otua Blank

**VADER'S NOTES:** "Seems to have a personal grudge against Luke's pal, Han Solo. Might give me a discount on hunting both of them down."

IG-88 is the one exception to the cantina's "no droids" policy

Spaceport cantinas are a great place for bounty hunters to pick up work

## AURRA SING

**SKILLS:** Infiltration, hunting Jedi, avoiding sunburn

**PAST EMPLOYERS:** Count Dooku, Ziro the Hutt, the Hutt Council

**VADER'S NOTES:** "Former Jedi Padawan. I'll try not to hold it against her. Once tried to assassinate my wife. That one I do hold against her."

## BOSSK

**SKILLS:** Tracking, capturing prey, limb regeneration (the lucky lizard!)

**PAST EMPLOYERS:** Boba Fett, Otua Blank, Galactic Empire

**VADER'S NOTES:** "Really hates Wookiees. Says he can smell them out anywhere. I can definitely use that."

## UNKNOWN

**SKILLS:** Unknown

**PAST EMPLOYERS:** Unknown

**VADER'S NOTES:** "I have no idea who this guy is. I guess not every bounty hunter can be famous, huh?"

OH, BOY! IT'S SO GREAT HANGING OUT WITH YOU GUYS!

Pilot suit

ARE YOU KIDDING? I BAGGED MORE THAN THAT BEFORE BREAKFAST.

## BOBA FETT

**SKILLS:** Being awesome

**PAST EMPLOYERS:** Pretty much everybody

**VADER'S NOTES:** "Has a bad habit of disintegrating his bounties. I'll have to warn him about that."

## CAD BANE

**SKILLS:** Theft, betrayal, sabotage, kicking small animals

**PAST EMPLOYERS:** Darth Sidious, Count Dooku, Jabba the Hutt

**VADER'S NOTES:** "Bane will do any job, no matter how dirty, crooked or mean. But I don't trust him enough to hire him."

# IMPERIAL MIGHT

**HOW DO YOU TEACH** rebellious planets not to mess with your Empire? It's all about attitude. Intimidation, fear and overwhelming firepower assist Darth Sidious in keeping his subjects in line… and having some of the scariest-looking ships and personnel around doesn't hurt, either.

Habitat decks house crew and stormtrooper battalions

### BOSS ON THE BRIDGE
On the command bridge of the *Executor*, Vader looms high above his Imperial crew, who tend to their instruments in sunken pits and desperately hope to avoid the Dark Lord's attention, not to mention his wrath.

Dagger-like shape

Titanium-reinforced alusteel hull

### THE *EXECUTOR*
Darth Vader's personal flagship is the Super Star Destroyer *Executor*. Stretching twelve times the length of an ordinary Star Destroyer, it is armed with thousands of turbolaser and ion cannons, and carries multiple squadrons of TIE fighters. The only thing stronger is the hull of the Death Star.

### MEDITATION CHAMBER
A hard-working Sith Lord needs his personal space. Deep within the *Executor* is a sealed pod that allows Vader to safely remove his helmet and mask as he focuses his thoughts on his latest mission from his Master, the Emperor.

Command tower

NO, NO, NO! I KEEP TELLING YOU, IT'S CALLED EXECUTOR, NOT EXECUTIONER!

## FAILURE IS NOT AN OPTION
It isn't a good idea to get on Darth Vader's bad side. Unfortunately for his officers aboard the *Executor*, Vader doesn't really have a good side. If you ever make a mistake, don't apologise – just find another officer to take the blame!

Upper stabiliser wing

Angled cockpit

## ROYAL GUARDS
The crimson-cloaked Imperial Royal Guards are devoted to protecting the Emperor at all times. Every guard would gladly give his life in the service of his duty – though they would much prefer to give the lives of the Emperor's enemies, instead.

## IMPERIAL SHUTTLE
Amongst the Empire's many transport vessels is the three-winged shuttle. The Emperor uses this ship to travel to the unfinished second Death Star and frighten its crew into completing construction faster.

Side wings fold up for landing

Double blaster cannon

# BOBA FETT

**WHEN YOU NEED** somebody tracked down, call Boba Fett. He's the best bounty hunter around, famous for always catching his target. That's why, when Darth Vader offers a reward for finding Luke Skywalker and his rebel friends, Boba Fett is on the job.

Targeting rangefinder

Mandalorian helmet

EE-3 carbine rifle

## BOUNTY HUNTER GEAR

The best bounty hunter needs the best equipment. Boba Fett is protected by an armoured chest plate and helmet, and he carries a variety of weapons and useful tools – some visible, and others hidden. He can even fly by using his jetpack.

Wookiee braid from a former bounty

Z-6 jetpack with grappling hook

Knee pad with hidden rocket dart launchers

## HATRED OF THE JEDI

Boba Fett is the cloned son of the legendary Jango Fett, a Mandalorian bounty hunter who worked for the Sith. Jango met his end at the hand of Jedi Master Mace Windu on the planet Geonosis. The young Boba swore revenge on the Jedi, and he has undertaken missions for the dark side ever since.

Spike-toed boots

## EMPLOYERS

Boba Fett's services are not cheap, so he is most often hired by the Empire and wealthy criminals such as Jabba the Hutt. He collects a double bounty on Han Solo by first locating him for Darth Vader, and then delivering him frozen in carbonite to Jabba!

When **Darth Vader** hired **Boba Fett** to locate the starship, the **Millennium Falcon**, Vader ordered him not to **disintegrate** the rebels on board.

> ❝ I CAN SEE WHY THEY CALL YOU THE BEST BOUNTY HUNTER IN THE GALAXY. ❞
> DARTH VADER

Pilot seat rotates for take-off and landing

Rotating wing

### SLAVE I
Fett's signature spacecraft once belonged to his father, Jango. The former police vehicle has been heavily modified with upgraded weaponry, engines and tracking systems. With Boba Fett at the controls, *Slave I* is almost impossible to outmanoeuvre or outrun.

Blaster cannons

Cargo hold

Flip-out missile launcher

## DATA FILE

- 🌐 **HOMEWORLD:** KAMINO
- 📅 **BIRTH DATE:** 31 BBY
- 🎖 **RANK:** BOUNTY HUNTER
- 👤 **TRAINED BY:** JANGO FETT
- 🔫 **WEAPON:** EE-3 CARBINE RIFLE

### A FITTING END
Boba Fett takes on one mission too many. In an attempt to keep Luke Skywalker and his friends from escaping Jabba's clutches, he falls into the Great Pit of Carkoon on Tatooine and is swallowed whole by the hungry Sarlacc beast inside.

WHOA! ANYBODY GOT A BREATH MINT?

# IMPERIAL FLEET

IT'S A COLOURFUL galaxy out there… and Darth Sidious doesn't like that one bit. That's why he builds his Empire's fleet in orderly shades of black, white and lots of grey. It gives everything a nice, unified look, and it makes his ships so much easier to keep clean.

## SUPER STAR DESTROYER
Darth Vader's gargantuan battle cruiser.
**SIZE** 19 km (12 miles) long
**SPEED** 40 megalight (MGLT)
**CAPACITY** 320,000 crew and personnel
**WEAPONS** Turbolaser batteries, ion cannons, laser cannons, concussion missiles

Intimidating dagger shape

Command bridge tower

## STAR DESTROYER
Massive, mile-long warships.
**SIZE** 16 km (1 mile) long
**SPEED** 60 MGLT
**CAPACITY** 47,000 crew and personnel
**WEAPONS** Turbolaser turrets, ion cannons

Turbolaser turret

Solar array wing

Transparisteel viewport

## TIE FIGHTER
Standard twin ion engine combat starfighter.
**SIZE** 8.99 m (29.5 feet) long
**SPEED** 100 MGLT
**CAPACITY** 1 pilot
**WEAPONS** 2 laser cannons

## TIE INTERCEPTOR
A faster and deadlier version of the TIE fighter.
**SIZE** 9.6 m (31.5 feet) long
**SPEED** 111 MGLT
**CAPACITY** 1 pilot
**WEAPONS** 4 laser cannons

## TIE ADVANCED
Darth Vader's prototype personal starfighter.
**SIZE** 9.2 m (30 feet) long
**SPEED** 105 MGLT
**CAPACITY** 1 pilot
**WEAPONS** 2 laser cannons, cluster missiles

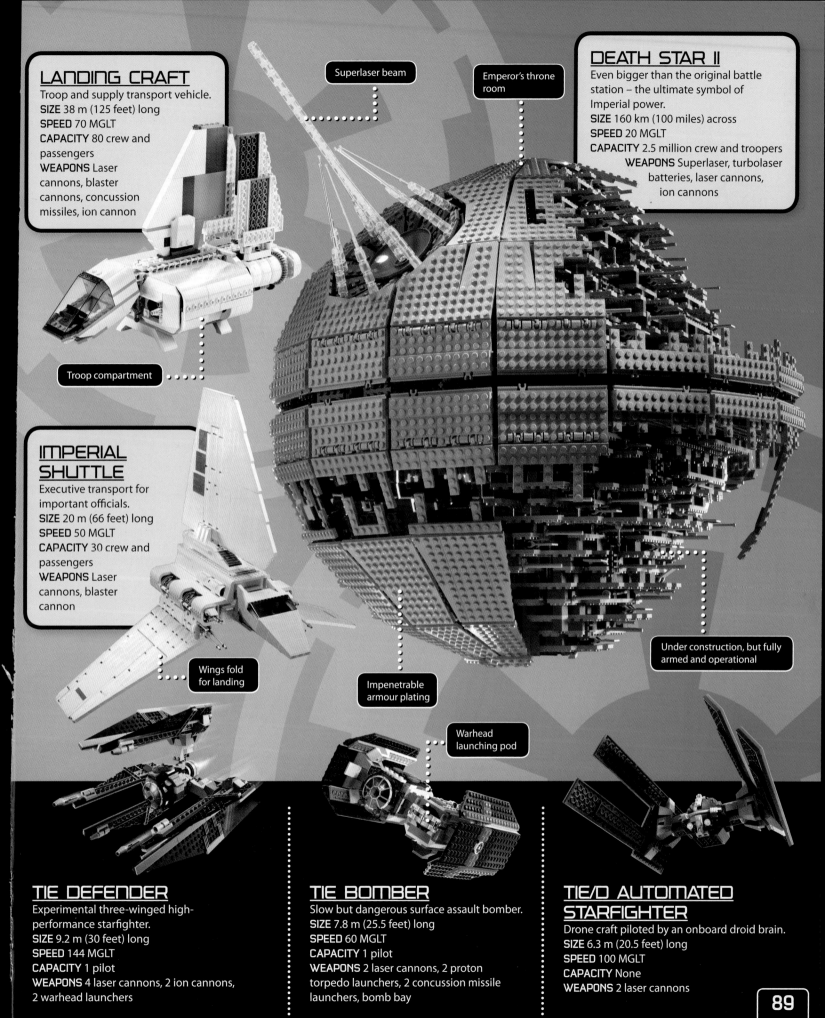

## LANDING CRAFT
Troop and supply transport vehicle.
**SIZE** 38 m (125 feet) long
**SPEED** 70 MGLT
**CAPACITY** 80 crew and passengers
**WEAPONS** Laser cannons, blaster cannons, concussion missiles, ion cannon

Troop compartment

Superlaser beam

Emperor's throne room

## DEATH STAR II
Even bigger than the original battle station – the ultimate symbol of Imperial power.
**SIZE** 160 km (100 miles) across
**SPEED** 20 MGLT
**CAPACITY** 2.5 million crew and troopers
**WEAPONS** Superlaser, turbolaser batteries, laser cannons, ion cannons

## IMPERIAL SHUTTLE
Executive transport for important officials.
**SIZE** 20 m (66 feet) long
**SPEED** 50 MGLT
**CAPACITY** 30 crew and passengers
**WEAPONS** Laser cannons, blaster cannon

Wings fold for landing

Impenetrable armour plating

Under construction, but fully armed and operational

Warhead launching pod

## TIE DEFENDER
Experimental three-winged high-performance starfighter.
**SIZE** 9.2 m (30 feet) long
**SPEED** 144 MGLT
**CAPACITY** 1 pilot
**WEAPONS** 4 laser cannons, 2 ion cannons, 2 warhead launchers

## TIE BOMBER
Slow but dangerous surface assault bomber.
**SIZE** 7.8 m (25.5 feet) long
**SPEED** 60 MGLT
**CAPACITY** 1 pilot
**WEAPONS** 2 laser cannons, 2 proton torpedo launchers, 2 concussion missile launchers, bomb bay

## TIE/D AUTOMATED STARFIGHTER
Drone craft piloted by an onboard droid brain.
**SIZE** 6.3 m (20.5 feet) long
**SPEED** 100 MGLT
**CAPACITY** None
**WEAPONS** 2 laser cannons

# HOW FAR WILL DARTH VADER GO TO RECRUIT HIS SON?

THERE IS NOTHING so terrible or evil that the ruthless Darth Vader will not do it to achieve his goals. He will capture spaceships, take over cities and blow up entire planets. When he discovers that the rebel pilot Luke Skywalker is his son, he pursues the young hero all across the galaxy. But what is Vader willing to do to turn Luke to the dark side?

Maintenance gantry

## A DEADLY PLAN
Darth Vader knows that Luke is a loyal friend. The Sith Lord captures Luke's fellow rebels on Cloud City, knowing that Luke will race to the rescue. Vader engages Luke in a fierce lightsaber duel – Luke must use all of his Jedi skill to avoid defeat.

Atmosphere sensor

## THE SECRET
Darth Vader is willing to do anything to get Luke to join him, even expose his deepest secret. During a ferocious battle, Vader batters Luke with Force-hurled objects, and even cuts off Luke's hand. Finally, with Luke cornered above a deep shaft, Vader reveals that he is Luke's father. The Sith Lord invites his son to join him in ruling the galaxy.

JOIN ME, LUKE, AND YOU CAN HAVE A COOL BLACK OUTFIT, TOO.

Support arm

Pipes severed by lightsaber

After the **battle** of the first **Death Star**, Vader was very **surprised** to **learn** the name of the rebel **pilot** who had destroyed it.

## DIFFICULT CHOICE
Luke proves himself to be a strong Jedi. He remains loyal to the Jedi code and refuses his father's offer. With no other way out, he drops into the shaft and is sucked through a gas port to the outside of the floating city. Luke is rescued by his friends aboard the *Millennium Falcon* and flown away.

I CAN GET ONE OF THOSE ON MY OWWNNN!

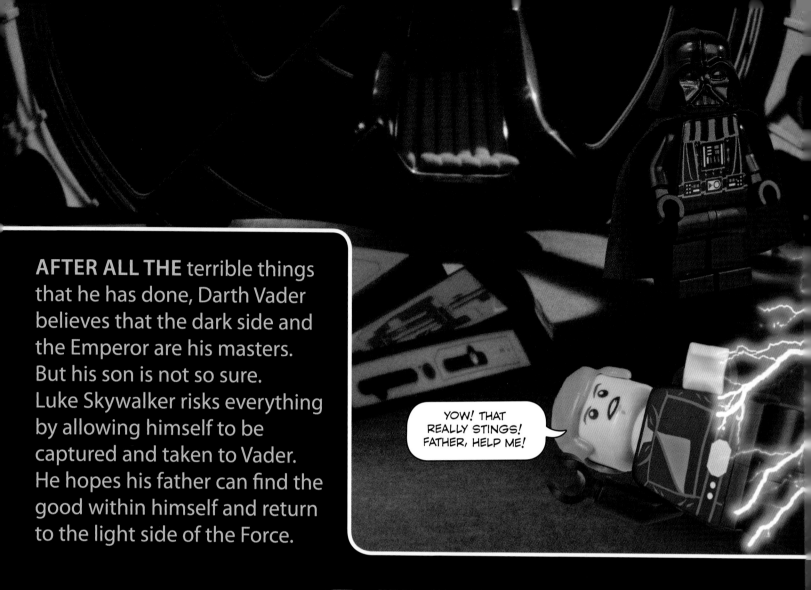

AFTER ALL THE terrible things that he has done, Darth Vader believes that the dark side and the Emperor are his masters. But his son is not so sure. Luke Skywalker risks everything by allowing himself to be captured and taken to Vader. He hopes his father can find the good within himself and return to the light side of the Force.

YOW! THAT REALLY STINGS! FATHER, HELP ME!

# CAN A SITH LORD

THAT'S IT, VADER. YOU'RE FIRED!

## THE FINAL SITH
As Darth Vader sees his son in danger, something awakens deep inside him. He seizes the Emperor and hurls him down the Death Star's reactor shaft. Darth Sidious is no more – but his Sith lightning has damaged Vader's life-support systems.

## LIGHTNING STRIKE

Vader is a remorseless Sith Lord, yet he still feels a connection to his son. Vader brings Luke to the Emperor aboard the second Death Star, but Luke refuses to turn to the dark side. In a rage, the Emperor attacks him with deadly Force lightning! Vader's feelings about Luke grow stronger, and he wonders whether a part of Anakin remains alive after all.

NEVER GONNA HAPPEN, KID!

By destroying the **Emperor** once and for all, Anakin finally fulfils the **prophecy** that said he would one day bring **balance** to the **Force.**

# BE REDEEMED?

### FROM SITH TO JEDI

Darth Vader has lived under a mask for 23 years. Reunited with the light side of the Force, he asks Luke to remove his helmet so he can see out of Anakin's eyes once more. Anakin passes on, asking Luke to tell Leia that Luke was right about their father's goodness all along.

### ONE WITH THE FORCE

When a noble Jedi departs from the physical world, he becomes one with the Force. As Luke burns Vader's armour on a pyre on the forest moon of Endor, he sees the spirits of three old friends: Obi-Wan Kenobi, Yoda and Anakin Skywalker – Jedi Knight.

# GLOSSARY

**ARCHDUKE**
Title given to the ruler of the planet Geonosis.

**BOUNTY HUNTER**
Someone who is hired to track down or destroy people or objects for money.

**CHANCELLOR**
The title given to the head of the Republic.

**CHOSEN ONE**
A person spoken of in an old Jedi prophecy who will bring balance to the Force.

**CLONE WARS**
A series of galaxy-wide battles fought between the Republic's Clone Army and the Separatist Droid Army, which took place between 22 and 19 BBY.

**CORUSCANT**
The capital of the Republic – and later, the Empire. This planet is home to the Senate and the Jedi Temple.

**CYBERNETIC**
Something that is half mechanical, half biological.

**CYBORG**
A being that is partly a living organism and partly a robot.

**DEATH STAR**
An enormous Imperial battle station, which has enough firepower to destroy an entire planet.

**EMPEROR**
Ruler of the Empire.

**EMPIRE**
A tyrannical power that rules the galaxy under the leadership of Emperor Palpatine, a Sith Lord.

**FORCE**
The energy that flows through all living things. It can be used for good or evil.

**FORCE LIGHTNING**
Deadly rays of blue energy used as a weapon.

**FORCE PUSH**
A blast of energy that a Force-user can use to knock over an opponent.

**HYPERDRIVE**
A component in a starship that allows it to travel faster than the speed of light.

**HYPERSPACE**
An extra dimension of space, used by experienced starship pilots to travel faster than the speed of light using a hyperdrive.

**JEDI**
A member of the Jedi Order who studies the light side of the Force.

**JEDI COUNCIL**
Twelve senior Jedi who meet to make important decisions.

**JEDI KNIGHT**
A full member of the Jedi Order who has completed his or her training.

**JEDI GRAND MASTER**
The head of the Jedi Order and the greatest and wisest of the Jedi Masters.

**JEDI MASTER**
An experienced and high-ranking Jedi who has demonstrated great skill and dedication.

**JEDI ORDER**
An ancient organisation that promotes peace and justice throughout the galaxy.

**JEDI TEMPLE**
The headquarters of the Jedi Order, located on the planet Coruscant.

**KYBER CRYSTAL**
A type of crystal harvested from ice caves on the planet Ilum for use in lightsabers.

**LIGHTSABER**
A sword-like weapon with a blade of pure energy that is used by Jedi and Sith.

**LIVING FORCE**
The view that the Force is present in all living things. Those who live by this view rely on their instincts and live in the moment.

**ORDER 66**
An order given by Chancellor Palpatine during the Clone Wars. Every clone trooper in the Clone Army was ordered to destroy all members of the Jedi Order.

**PADAWAN**
A young Jedi apprentice who is in training to become a fully fledged Jedi Knight.

**REBEL ALLIANCE**
The organisation that resists and fights the Empire.

**REPUBLIC**
The democratic government that rules many planets in the galaxy.

**SENATE**
The government of the Republic. It is made up of senators from all over the galaxy.

**SEPARATISTS**
An alliance of those who are opposed to the Republic.

**SITH**
An ancient sect of Force-sensitives who seek to use the dark side of the Force to gain power.

**TRADE FEDERATION**
A bureaucratic organisation that controls much of the trade and commerce in the galaxy.

**VICEROY**
The leader of the Trade Federation.

**WOOKIEE**
Tall, hairy creatures from the planet Kashyyyk who usually oppose the dark side.

INDEX

LONDON, NEW YORK, MELBOURNE,
MUNICH AND DELHI

| | |
|---|---|
| Editor | **Shari Last** |
| Designers | **Jon Hall and Rhys Thomas** |
| Additional Designers | **Julie Thompson and Mark Richards** |
| Pre-Production Producer | **Siu Yin Chan** |
| Senior Producer | **Lloyd Robertson** |
| Managing Editor | **Elizabeth Dowsett** |
| Design Manager | **Ron Stobbart** |
| Publishing Manager | **Julie Ferris** |
| Art Director | **Lisa Lanzarini** |
| Publishing Director | **Simon Beecroft** |

Additional photography by Gary Ombler.

Dorling Kindersley would like to thank Randi Sørensen and Robert Stefan Ekblom
at the LEGO Group; J. W. Rinzler, Chris Gollaher, Leland Chee, Troy Alders
and Carol Roeder at Lucasfilm; and Jo Casey for editorial assistance.

First published in Great Britain in 2014
by Dorling Kindersley Limited
80 Strand, London WC2R 0RL

10 9 8 7 6 5 4 3 2
004—195848—Sep/14

Page design copyright © 2014 Dorling Kindersley Limited
A Penguin Random House Company

A CIP catalogue record for this book
is available from the British Library.

ISBN: 978-1-40934-738-5

Colour reproduction by Alta Image, UK
Printed and bound in China by Leo Paper Products, Ltd.

Discover more at
**www.dk.com**
**www.LEGO.com/starwars**
**www.starwars.com**